D1262026

YOU **HAVEN'T SEEN** ANYTHING YET
SERMONS FOR ADVENT, CHRISTMAS, EPIPHANY

YOU HAVEN'T SEEN ANYTHING YET

SERMONS FOR ADVENT, CHRISTMAS, EPIPHANY

MARK TROTTER   **CYCLE B GOSPEL TEXTS**

C.S.S. Publishing Co., Inc.
Lima, Ohio

Library of Congress Cataloging-in-Publication Data

Trotter, Mark.
    You haven't seen anything yet / Mark Trotter
        p.   cm.
    ISBN 1-55673-219-8
    1. Advent sermons.   2. Christmas sermons.   3. Epiphany season —
Sermons.   4. Sermons, American.   I. Title.
BV40.T76   1990
252'.61--dc20   9033590
                                                                          CIP

9031 / ISBN 1-55673-219-8   PRINTED IN U.S.A.

Contents

You Haven't Seen Anything Yet

Advent 1   *Mark 13:32-37*

This is the First Sunday in Advent, the time of preparation for Christmas. The church has always prepared for Christmas by getting back to biblical times, back to the time of Israel, the time before Christ's coming, to experience what it was like to wait for a Messiah.

That's the mood of the Advent hymns.

> *O come, O come Emmanuel,*
> *And ransom captive Israel,*
> *That mourns in lonely exile here*
> *Until the Son of God appear.*

The hymn captures the mood of Advent; a time of expectation, a time of not-having, a time of waiting on God to act, as in the time before Christ's first coming, the time of ancient Israel.

Advent is also a time that reminds us that when God did act, it was not as expected. Listen to Handel's *Messiah*, the texts he chose from the Old Testament prophecies of the

7

Messiah, and you can hear about what kind of Messiah Israel expected.

> *Who shall stand on the day of His coming,*
> *for He is like a refiner's fire?*
>
> *For thus saith the Lord, "I will shake the*
> *heavens and the earth, the sea and the dry*
> *land, and all nations I will shake."*

They expected a Messiah to come "as a refiner's fire" in judgment; instead they got a baby, lying in a manger. They expected darkness; instead they got light.

The purpose of Advent is to get you to experience that, to see what it is like "to wait in lonely exile here until the Son of God appear." There is a reason for that. If you can experience what it was like for Israel to wait for the Messiah, then perhaps you will see that that is what you are doing now. Advent is not only the remembrance of a time back then, but a description of human life now. To the extent that our life is a time of waiting, this, too, is Advent.

Have you ever asked, "If the Messiah has come, why doesn't the world look like the Kingdom of God?" Or perhaps you have asked, or had somebody ask you, "If Christianity has been around for 2,000 years, why isn't the world more Christian?" Why aren't the Christians more Christian? Why this gap between the promise and the result? Why the distance between what I had hoped for in my life and what my life has actually been? Christ has come! That's what Christmas is all about, and yet the world is not the way it should be, not the way the prophecies said it would be.

In Advent we look honestly at the distance between what is promised and what has actually happened, what ought to be and what really is. The church's answer to the hard questions of Advent is, "Christ has come and Christ will come again." In the meantime we, like Israel, must wait.

O come, O come, Emmanuel,
And ransom captive Israel,
That mourns in lonely exile here
Until the Son of God appear.

We're not just role playing when we sing that. We're not just pretending that we are back in the time before the first Christmas. We are singing about ourselves, about our own lives. We are singing about a world that still has Herods in it, where people are still poor and homeless, where there are wars and rumors of wars, sickness and pain, absurd suffering and dying. It is still a world in which people cry out for justice; still they cry for some meaning and purpose in their lives; still they cry for someone to save them from their sins, or to save them from the consequences of the sins of others.

If you can see the gap between what has been promised at Christmas and the way the world is now, and have asked the hard question, "Where is God in all of this?" then you know why the early church prayed, "Come quickly, Lord Jesus." And why they sang, "Christ has come; Christ will come again." And why they recited, "I believe in Jesus Christ . . . who ascended into heaven . . . and from thence he shall come to judge the quick and the dead." And most of all, you will understand why they remembered all those things Jesus himself said about his coming again, and why they included them in their Holy Scriptures: so they would always be there to provide answers for these hard questions.

Our text for this week is one such passage. It answers two Advent questions: When will Jesus return? And, what are we to do in the meantime? Listen to the passage in that light:

But of that day or that hour no one knows, not even the angels in heaven, nor the Son, but only the Father. Take heed, watch; for you do not know when the time will come.

> *It is like a man going on a journey, when he leaves home and puts his servants in charge, each with his work, and commands the doorkeeper to be on the watch. Watch therefore — for you do not know when the Master of the house will come, in the evening, or at midnight, or at cockcrow, or in the morning — lest he come suddenly and find you asleep. And what I say to you I say to all: Watch.*

The message is clear. Those who wait for the Second Coming are not to speculate on when it will come or how it will come. The passage reverberates with what Paul Scherer called the "agnostic note." We do not know. Three times it is underscored. Three times it says the same thing: "Of that hour and that time nobody knows." "For you do not know when the time will come." "For you do not know when the Master will come." Three times in a passage of five verses it says, "You do not know . . ." It says it so many times everybody ought to get it.

Apparently I am wrong because there are still people who think that they can know when it will happen. They connect any prophecy they want in the Bible with any event they want in the modern world. Maybe they do that because there is something in human nature that wants to hear bad news, that wants to hear that we are always on the brink of disaster. Some people want the daily news delivered to them in apocalyptic language. They are consumers of catastrophe. They read current events as if these are the last days.

I'll bet you this: Somebody will take the most recent stock market decline, connect it to the visit of a Communist leader to this country, throw in a few California earthquakes, and conclude, "This is it. These are the last days. He is coming. It's right there in the Bible."

Well, it may or may not be. I don't know. But I do know that the agnostic note in the Bible says that nobody else knows either. Nobody! Not the angels, or even the Son. So don't speculate. The agnostic note appears three times in five verses so that even the dullest among us ought to get it. Nobody knows the hour or time, when or how. So don't worry about it.

But it does say somebody knows, and this is the most important part of this text. This is the good news. It says you don't know about these things, but God knows, and that's all that you need to know.

You see, when it comes to the future, it's like that advice about being a success, "It's not what you know, it's who you know." You may not know what's up, but God knows, and that's all you need to know. "No one knows not even the angels in heaven, not the Son, but only the Father."

It is no accident that Jesus chose that word "Father." It's the most personal word used for God, *Abba*. It's the one he told us to use when we pray, "our Father." No one knows the future but the Father. That's to suggest that we are to be like children regarding the future. In relation to the future, we are all like children.

I remember what it was like being the father of four small children, how they put their trust in me. It came as a terrible realization that my children had absolute faith in me. They didn't worry about the future. That was my problem; they left that up to me. They lived one day at a time. My question was, "What's going to happen tomorrow?" Their question was, "What are we doing today?" They would bring questions to me, confident that no matter what the question, no matter how difficult, I would be able to answer it. They would make a statement to somebody else, turn to me and ask, "Isn't that right?" as if I knew the answer to everything.

They'd even bring their broken toys to me to fix, confident that I could fix all things. I remember their bewilderment when I couldn't fix all things. I'd tell them, "of course, nobody could fix this, not the angels in heaven, nor the Son . . . nobody." They would believe that, too.

I remember our summers in the woods, in an unfamiliar, wild land, comparatively speaking, filled with real danger. The most imminent danger was getting lost, so their parents set boundaries beyond which they could not go. They could not go to the river. They could not go into the woods. They could go down to the stream, but not cross the stream. That parental warning was sufficient to put in them the fear of this mysterious perimeter around their lives. They never trespassed it.

But when their father or mother would go with them to the river, or into the woods, they would go without hesitation, without fear, the bravest running ahead on the trail, out of sight, but never out of sound of the father's voice.

"No one knows but the Father" means we are to be like children in relation to the future. That is to say, we are asked to move into the unknown in life, trusting that the God who has brought us this far will not abandon us. Even though we cannot see him, he knows us. That's why Jesus said, "No one knows but the Father." And that's all we need to know.

And then that word, "watch." It answers the second question. The first question was: "When will the Messiah come?" The answer was, "No one knows but the Father." The second question is: "Then what are we to do?" And the answer is, we are to watch.

The phrase "No one knows" appears three times in five verses. "Watch" also appears three times in the same five verses, including the last word, for emphasis. "What I say to you, I say to all: Watch."

Couched in the middle of the passage is the parable of the doorkeeper to reveal what it means to watch. The master goes away and leaves his servants with work to do and assigns only the doorkeeper to do the watching.

So, according to the parable, to be watchful means to work, to be doing what the master told you to do, and not to worry about when he will come back. Just worry about what you are supposed to do. You've got enough to do to keep you busy in the present without engaging in idle speculation about the future. And you know what he told you to do. He told you to feed the hungry, heal the sick, house the homeless, befriend the stranger, give the enemy a cup of cold water, and love your neighbor. That's what you are supposed to do. Watching looks like work.

In that sense we can learn from our cousins in biblical religion, the Jews. They are experts in watching. They have a long history of instruction in how to wait for the Messiah. We can learn from them.

There is a legend about Johanan Ben Akkai, a pupil of the famous rabbi, Hillel. Akkai said to his pupils, "If you are planting a tree and you hear that the Messiah has come, finish planting the tree, then go and inquire." That fits perfectly with Jesus' teaching that watching means working. You do not know when the Master will return. Nobody knows. So keep on working. So far all of the predictions have been false. No one knows. So keep on working. Do the work of the Lord, and watch.

There is another wonderfully hopeful note in this passage. The fact that we don't know about the future means that we can be infinitely hopeful. It is possible, in fact it is likely, that his second coming will be as unpredictable and as marvelous a surprise as the first.

I came across some fascinating information about chess in the writings of Martin Marty. There are 400 possible positions after each player has made one move. After each player has made the second move, there are over 70,000 possible positions. After three moves, there are more than 9,000,000. I would have thought it quite the opposite. I would have thought that the greatest number of possibilities existed before you did anything, and the longer you played, the fewer the options. But the fact is, the more moves, the greater the options.

The same is true of the future, which is why Jesus told us not to worry about it. Just keep praying. Just keep working. Just keep doing your best. The more you do, the greater the possibilities that God can do something.

Then this occurred to me: Maybe the word "watch" has a different meaning than what we have given it. Maybe it doesn't mean to watch with eyes squinted to see the signs of the end. Maybe it doesn't mean anxious eyes scanning the horizon in order to see if an enemy is coming. I always thought that this was what the watchman was for, to give us a warning so that we could brace ourselves, get under cover.

But maybe "watch" in Advent doesn't mean that at all. Maybe "watch" means: Look at this! Or, you haven't seen anything yet! Now, watch! The way a magician will get our attention, get us to watch him closely, examine his sleeves. And then he will do something absolutely dazzling, something that we wouldn't ever expect to have happened, not in this world.

Maybe that's how we are to apply Advent to our contemporary lives. "Watch" means, "Watch this." You think a baby born in a manger was something? Well, watch this.

What I say to you, I say to all. You just watch!

You Have to Start Someplace

Advent 2

Mark 1:1-8

You ask anyone in the New Testament how you get to Bethlehem, and they will say, "Go out to the desert, keep going till you get to the River Jordan. You can't miss it. You'll find a man out there, standing knee deep in the water, baptizing people. That's John the Baptizer. You ask him. If you want to go to Bethlehem, you've got to start there. There is no other way to get there."

They all say the same thing, all four gospels: Matthew, Mark, Luke and John. They all say that if you want to go to Bethlehem, you've got to start with John the Baptizer.

Our text this Second Sunday of Advent is the first words in the Gospel of Mark.

> *The beginning of the gospel of Jesus Christ, the Son of God. Behold I send my messenger, John the Baptizer.*

That's the way Mark begins his gospel. Of course, Mark doesn't say anything about Bethlehem. In fact, Mark doesn't have a birth narrative; he doesn't even mention it. But he still starts with John. At the beginning of the Gospel of Jesus Christ, according to Mark, there is John the Baptizer.

You've got to start somewhere, right? All the gospels say you have to start with John the Baptizer. Even those gospels that don't record Christmas stories, Mark and John, begin with John the Baptizer.

The Gospel of John begins with these beautiful words: "In the beginning was the Word and the Word was with God, and the Word was God." John uses wonderfully lofty, aesthetically beautiful language. John is very Greek, with his *logos*, the Greek term we translate "word," but was really the "principle of creation," the power that created all things. In the beginning was the *logos*.

John also records Jesus delivering long discourses, as if he were a Greek philosopher. The Gospel of John is sophisticated in its style, so very Greek. And yet John, like all the others, begins with John the Baptizer, the old Jewish prophet, the man who ate locusts and wild honey, dressed in animal skins. Five verses into this sophisticated gospel there he is: "there was a man sent from God whose name was John."

You can't get away from him. You have to start this journey to Bethlehem with John.

It looks like Matthew might be the exception. Matthew begins with the story of the birth of Jesus. Matthew waits until the third chapter to introduce John the Baptizer. Perhaps he got carried away telling the wonderful stories about Joseph and his dreams and the visit of the wise men, because there is no mention of John in the first two chapters. It appears in Matthew that you can make it to Bethlehem and back without running into him. Not quite. Out of nowhere he appears at the start of the third chapter. As you leave the stable of Bethlehem, John is waiting, leaning against the fence, greeting you as you come out of the door. He's a little late, but he made it. The third chapter begins, "In those days came John the Baptizer preaching, "Repent!' "

He's always there. In all of the gospels. He's right there at the beginning.

Luke presents the most familiar and most popular of all of the Christmas stories. Get this: Luke begins his gospel not with the story of the birth of Jesus, but with a fully developed story of the birth of John the Baptizer.

What's more, Luke says that Elizabeth, who is John's mother, and Mary, the mother of Jesus, were cousins. He says they got together when they were both pregnant, sang together, shared stories, talked about what all of this meant.

I just point this out to you: If instead of relying on the shopping malls and the television specials to tell you what Christmas is about, you turn to the Bible, you are going to run into John the Baptizer. John is there in every story, out on the desert, standing in the River Jordan, telling us how to get to Bethlehem . . . from here.

I don't know about you, but I don't want to go out there, because I know what John is going to say. He says only one thing, you know, like a broken record. What kind of a preacher is it who has only one sermon? No wonder he's out there in the desert. The bishop probably sent him out there. You know what his one sermon is? "Repent!" He doesn't soften it with jokes. He doesn't gild it with poetry. He just roars like a lion in the wilderness. You can hear his roar an hour before you see him. You can hear "Repent!" echoing off the barren landscape. I don't want to hear that.

Years ago I was excited about going to a new church, a new town, a new job. After I was there for several months I had physical symptoms I thought I'd better do something about. I chose a doctor I had known for years. I had gone to college with him. He was a good friend back in those days, so I thought he would be gentle, merciful, and kind.

He put me through all those tests, sat me down in his office, and said, "There is nothing physically wrong with you. You're in great shape. Your problem is that you are anxious.

Now," he said, "we have two options. I can give you some pills, or you can practice what you preach."

I never went back to him. I knew what he would say to me if I went back. He would say, "Have you started practicing what you preach?" I don't want to hear that.

John the Baptizer is the same way. He has one question. I know what it is. I know he's going to say, "Have you started practicing what you believe?" And I don't want to hear that, especially at this time of year.

You see, John is a prophet. Some people think that a prophet is somebody who can foretell the future. That's probably because "prophecy" in English refers to predicting the future, and that's part of what prophets do. That part is easy to take. What is hard to take is what prophets say about the present. What they say about the present is "Repent!" — which means practice what you preach.

Prophets rarely say anything new; they rarely disclose any new information. They tell you what you already know but don't want to be reminded of. They tell you to start living what you believe.

And one more thing about prophets: they never say the "right thing." The right thing is what the right people, the people with power, want to hear. Prophets are always going to the right people and saying the wrong thing, the thing that they don't want to hear. All the biblical prophets did that, including John the Baptizer. And all of them suffered for it, including John.

John goes to Herod the King, who thought himself to be liberated from common decency. King Herod had committed adultery, incest, murder, and God knows what else. John the Baptizer went to Herod and said, "Shape up! Your lifestyle is going to bring down the whole nation!"

The Jews had this idea that morality is serious business. And what's more, they said, it's not private business. It's corporate business. What you do is not your own business, not even if you are a king or a queen. What you do, or what you do not do, will either hurt or bless somebody else. Society is not made up of autonomous individuals, moral virtuosos, each one doing his or her own thing. Life is not like a circus filled with performers. Life is like an expedition.It's like going on a journey. It's like a pilgrimage. It's like ascending a mountain, each one tied to the other, where we need each other. Where, if one is sick or injured, or one is uncooperative, or wasteful, or bellicose, everybody suffers.

Prophets are always reminding the people of that. You will never hear a prophet shout, "Do your own thing!" Prophets shout, "Do what God has told you to do. You know what it is. Now do it!" And that's when they get into trouble, everyone of them. John the Baptizer did with Herod. Herod won that fight. John the Baptizer lost his head over it.

When Jesus heard what had happened to John, what Herod had done to him, do you know what he said? "There is no man born of woman greater than John." That's high praise coming from Jesus. Jesus knew John. Luke says they are cousins. Jesus held John in the highest regard. The respect was mutual. You know what John said of Jesus? "The one who comes after me is greater than I am, the thong of whose sandals I am not worthy to stoop down to untie."

I don't know of any relationship quite like that in the Bible, this mutual respect, this clear delineation of roles, this sense that we are a team, what I do is preparation for you, what I do is fulfillment for you. We could put it this way: Jesus said, "No one born of woman is greater than John the Baptizer. Listen to him." John said, "Jesus is the one you are waiting for. Follow him."

They all say the same thing, all four gospels. They all say, if you want to go to Bethlehem to see for yourself, if you want to find out who Jesus really is, then first go see John.

So we might as well do it. We might as well get it over with. John says just what you would expect. He says it right off. "Repent! Practice what you preach! Live up to the standards that you believe in. You know what they are. Do it."

That's what repentance means. Repentance doesn't mean going through life with your head down, feeling remorseful for being so bad. It means start doing something good. Start practicing what you believe in.

But why do we have to hear that at Christmas time? That's the question I ask, and it has been asked of me many times. I have been preaching now for over twenty-five years, and every Advent I have to preach the story of John the Baptizer, so I decided this year I'm going to ask him, "John, how come you keep talking about repentance at Christmas time? I mean, can't you get into the spirit? No wonder you're not on any Christmas cards. You are in danger of being the *Grinch Who Stole Christmas*. This is a happy time. It's party time. This is not a gloomy time."

Old John comes out of the water. He's been in there so long that his legs are blue. He says, "You fixin' to go to Bethlehem?" I say, "Yes, we're on our way there. We'll be there in about two weeks." He says, "Well, let me tell you what happened out there. Let me tell you what's at stake. What happened out there at Bethlehem is nothing less than an invasion, not a violent one with armies, but a quiet one with love. A beachhead for the Kingdom of God.

"Not many people believe that because it's not what they had expected, nor is it what they want. But that's the way it happened anyway. I believe that. I believe that the Kingdom of God is now here. The Kingdom of God is now set against the kingdoms of this world, and now you've got to choose. You've got to choose which kingdom you are going to give your loyalty to — the Kingdom of God or the kingdom of this world. Are you going to give your loyalty to Herod or to Christ? And when you make up your mind, then you come out to see me here and I'll tell you what you must do to really celebrate the meaning of Christmas."

Well, I knew he was going to say that. He says it every Advent and I didn't want to hear it. I wanted to hear that because God came into this world the way it is, the way it is is the way God likes it. But John won't let me get away with that. John says that God came into this world to change it, and that he wants to begin with me.

I want to hear that Christmas is just a good feeling, a time of make-believe. I want my Christmas celebration to be a respite from the hard facts of this world. I want it to be a time of carols, of good cheer, parties, and good food. I want it to be a reprieve from the real world. I want it to be like Muzak on the elevator, like mood music while we put the world on hold.

And John won't allow that. He says Christmas means nothing less than an invasion of this world by God, like the beachhead at Normandy. A new age is here. The Kingdom has come. There are two kingdoms now: Herod and his successors, Jesus and his disciples. You've got to make the choice. You've got to make the choice between the kingdom of Rome and the Kingdom of God, between the kingdom of iron and the Kingdom of Love. You've got to choose.

And then John walks back into the water of the river saying, "It's here all right. The Kingdom of God is here right now." He turns his head, and says over his shoulder, "And you know that it is here." Then he takes up his one note message: "Repent, for the Kingdom of God is at hand!"

You see, John is there every Advent in case, just in case, this is the year that you want to go to Bethlehem. "Repent" means start doing the things that you know you should do. If you are alienated from somebody, be reconciled. If you are self-righteous in relation to somebody, humble yourself. If you have been uncaring about the poor, now is the time to get some moral imagination and put yourself in the plight of another human being. If you have been callous about the prospects for peace in this world, now is the time for you to start praying and working for those things that make for peace. If you have put your trust in the accumulation of things so that you are slave to a whole host of masters, now is the time for you to unload some of that stuff and put your trust in God. And if you have assumed to this point that you are going to be judged on your ability to avoid evil in this life, Christmas is a time for you to hear that you are going to be judged on your courage to do the good.

So John is waiting. He's waiting there until you are ready to hear the real meaning of Christmas, until you are ready to see that what happened then is to make a difference in what happens now.

Stephen Vincent Benet wrote a Christmas play in which he pictured the wife of the innkeeper, who knows what momentous thing has happened back there in the barn, saying, "Something is loosed to change the shaken world, and with it we must change."

When you are ready to do that, John will be waiting.

You've Got the Wrong Man

Advent 3   *John 1:6-8, 19-28*

We are back with John the Baptizer again this week. Every gospel begins with John the Baptizer, because John is the one who prepares the way for the Messiah. John the Baptizer fulfills the prophecy: "A voice cries in the wilderness, prepare the way of the Lord." That's old John. He is the voice crying in the wilderness to shape up, repent, get ready for the coming of the Kingdom of God, the coming of the Messiah.

The Gospel of John puts John the Baptizer at the beginning of the gospel as well, but tells the story a little differently. John the Baptizer is still the voice, only he's not crying in the wilderness, "Repent!" He is the voice proclaiming testimony to who Jesus really is.

You see it in this fascinating scene in the first chapter. John the Baptizer is being interrogated by the authorities, as if he had been taken downtown for questioning. They got the wrong man. They thought John the Baptizer was the Messiah. That's what the Gospel of John wants you to see right off; John the Baptizer is not the Messiah. It was a case of mistaken identity. They got the wrong man.

It's understandable how the mistake could have happened. The word was out that the Messiah had come. If he had come, then he must have been around there someplace. So, where was he? Who is he? The obvious answer was John the Baptizer. He had to be the one. John was very religious. He renounced the things of this world. You could call John a religious fanatic. He ate grasshoppers and quaffed them down with wild honey! I can just see old John out in the desert sticking his hand in the beehive to get some honey.

John was eccentric, to say the least. But the people loved him. They saw in him the authenticity of the prophet, and they flocked to hear him. He was baptizing people in the River Jordan, and he tied his baptism to the Kingdom of God. That's another reason why they suspected John the Baptizer was the Messiah; he was preaching that the Kingdom of God is at hand. He was getting everybody ready for it.

That was the purpose of baptizing in the River Jordan. It was across the Jordan that their forbears had passed to enter the Promised Land centuries before. John is saying, go back to the beginning, back to the river Jordan, and cross over it again. Only this time, cross into the Kingdom of God.

It would be similar to Americans going back to the shores of New England, once again stepping onto the shore and renewing the Mayflower Compact. John was calling Israel to start over again, to go back to their beginnings and remember who they were, remember how God had called them. Wipe the slate clean. Repent! Get ready for the Kingdom of God!

That struck a responsive chord in the hearts of all of the people and they flocked to John. They loved John. They regarded him highly. Some even venerated him. And the authorities knew that. They knew that John was popular, and they knew what John was preaching, "The Kingdom of God is at hand!"

So when the word came to them, "There are those who are saying the Messiah is here," the authorities said, "It's got to be John the Baptizer. It couldn't be anybody else. All the evidence points to John the Baptizer."

And so, according to our text, they sent priests and Levites from Jerusalem, an intelligence unit, out to the desert beyond Bethany to John.

"Who are you?" they asked.

He confessed, "I am not the Christ." Notice that the word that is in the text is "confess," as if this were some legal proceeding. "I am not the Christ," he confessed.

Then they asked, "Are you Elijah?" This question is important because Elijah was to return just before the coming of the Messiah.

He said, "I am not Elijah."

They asked, "Are you not then the prophet?" The prophet was another expected forerunner of the Messiah.

He said, "No, I am not the prophet."

"Then who are you? Let us have an answer."

He said, "I am the voice crying in the wilderness, make straight the way of the Lord."

They said, "Then why are you baptizing if you are not the Christ, or Elijah, or the prophet?"

He said, "I baptize with water, but among you stands one whom you do not know, even he who comes after me, the thong of whose sandal I am not worthy to untie."

They got the wrong man. They thought it's got to be John. He's the only one that it could be. Look how popular he is. He's a celebrity. Everybody loves him. If they had one of those Harris polls that picks the most admired in the nation in a particular year, they would have picked John the Baptizer. It had to be him. So they asked him, "Are you the one?" He said, "No. But among you stands one whom you do not know."

That is our text. It's a marvelous text. It's also a disturbing text, because it sounds like the Messiah is hiding. "Among you stands one whom you don't know." Sounds like he's *incognito,* in disguise. What kind of Messiah is it whose presence is so inconspicuous that you don't know if he is here or not?

The Gospel of John says that John the Baptizer finally had to finger him, point him out to the authorities. That's in the next scene. John sees Jesus coming toward him, points and says, "Behold the Lamb of God who takes away the sins of the world." And from that time on the authorities tail Jesus until they get enough evidence to have him arrested.

But I wonder, would they ever have found him, would they have known who he was, if John hadn't squealed? He was here *incognito.* John knew who he was, but nobody else did. He was a most unlikely Messiah. He was born in a manger, not in a mansion. His parents were peasants, not royalty. He was raised in Nazareth, a little backwater place, not the capital, the cosmopolitan city of Jerusalem. You name the qualifications for the Messiah, and he didn't have them. There was nothing about him that would prompt anybody to suspect that he was the Messiah, or even take notice of him. That's why John the Baptizer said, "There stands among you one whom you don't even know."

Which is entirely consistent with the rest of the portrait, not only in John, but in the other gospels. John puts it this way. "He was in the world, but the world knew him not." "He went to his own home and his own people received him not." John says even his disciples didn't know him. Jesus says to Philip, "Have I been with you so long, and yet you do not know me?" Then he says, "A little while and you will see me no more. Again, a little while and you will see me." The disciples were bewildered. They asked, "What is he talking about? It sounds like, 'Now you see me, now you don't.' "

I want you to consider something. Think about this. What we have in these passages is nothing less than a revelation of God's *modus operandi.* "He stands among you as one unknown." That is the way that God works in our lives. It's not only the way God worked then; it's the way God works now.

So if you are at all suspicious, if you suspect that something is going on in your life, that something is happening around here, if you are on the lookout for God but haven't been able to find him, this is the way he works. Consider this. This is his *m.o.*

First of all God will appear *incognito*. That's clearly his way of operation. So don't expect flashes of light, chariots of fire, or opening skies. God doesn't work that way. That's not his *m.o.* That may be the reason why so many people have missed him. God has probably gotten in and out of their lives before they even suspected anything was going on. They never imagined that what happened to them was the work of God because they were looking for something really big, something supernatural, and that just is not the way that God works.

Now somebody is going to point out to me, "Of course, there are visions and epiphanies and the parting of the seas and the shaking of the mountains, the whole business. It's all there in the Bible." I know that. I know there is a whole lot of other stuff there in the Bible, too, but I wouldn't count on it happening to you if I were you. The hard evidence indicates that God will come into your life *incognito*. In fact, he may be in your neighborhood right now. He may have gotten by your Neighborhood Watch.

Now get this. He might even be here in church, of all places. Can you imagine that? He might even be here in this service today. There is a wonderful piece of evidence of this in the Gospel of Luke. It's after the Resurrection. Two men are walking down the road to Emmaus. They are joined by a stranger. They talk, the three of them, walking along. They come to an inn. The two invite the stranger to eat with them. They sit down at the table. They take the bread. It's him! They swear to it. It's him. They run to tell the disciples, "We saw him. He ate with us. And then he disappeared." Now you see him, now you don't. "Among you stands one whom you do not know."

And this similar story from the writing of Turgenev, the Russian writer. "Once we were all standing and waiting in church, when a man came up from behind and stood beside me. I did not turn towards him, but I felt the man was Christ. Emotion, curiosity, awe, over-mastered me. I made an effort and looked at my neighbor. A face like everyone's, a face like all men's faces. What sort of Christ is this, I thought. Such an ordinary man. It cannot be. I turned away, but I had hardly turned my eyes from this ordinary man when I felt with unshakable conviction that this was Christ standing beside me. Suddenly my heart sank, and only then I realized that such a face, like all men's faces, is the face of Christ. And just such feet, boots with real mud on them, are his."

"He stands among you as one whom you do not know." He may even be in church. There is a custom in some churches of greeting the person next to you. You may take that more seriously now. You may want to tidy up before you pass the peace.

"Among you stands one whom you do not know." God comes sometimes as a stranger. God comes often as a friend. So you never know. That's why you are to be prepared.

But this is the most decisive piece of evidence. This is the most consistent *modus operandi* that we have. We should be prepared to find him in circumstances that are humble, and among the poor. That's the most incredible evidence of all, and for many the most offensive, that when God took on our flesh, he took on poor flesh.

It's right there before your nose. Just look all around you, especially this time of year, the most popular holiday of the year, perhaps the most popular holiday in all of the world. The evidence is all about you that when God became a human being, he became an outcast. There was no room for him at the inn.

And of all people to be chosen to be the instrument of God's will for our salvation, it would be a humble peasant woman, now exalted above all women. A poor woman, Mary. Every creche in this Advent will place the evidence right there before your eyes. That's the meaning of the creche. The creche is a stable, a barn. That's where he came. When God came into this world he came into humble circumstances, and among the poor.

If you are on the lookout for him, then look for him there. He even told you to do that. Jesus said, "If you have done it unto the least of these, you have done it to me." That's where he will be, among the poor, the least, and the lowly.

But I think it means more than that. I think it means not only that the poor are to be the object of our charity, especially at this time of year; it also says that the poor have something to give to us. It's the quality that in the Bible is called "blessedness." "Blessed are the poor for theirs is the Kingdom of God."

I got a glimpse of what this means in Henry Nouwen's writing about his living in Peru. Nouwen is a Catholic priest, an expert on spirituality. He decided to give up his prominent teaching post at Yale and go serve the poor in South America. He worked as a priest in a parish of 100,000 believers outside Lima, Peru. Most of them were children, and most of them abjectly poor. He went there to help them, and he ended up being helped. He went there as a priest to present Christ to them — that's what a priest does — and he discovered that they presented Christ to him.

He said that wherever he went, the children were tugging at him, holding on to the fingers of his hands, playing with him, laughing. They were telling him something. "They were giving me the sense that this is a day that the Lord has made. Let us rejoice in it! This is a gift given to us. Let us be glad in it."

There were only three priests in this parish for 100,000 persons, so every night there was a Eucharist to which they invited people who had recently lost members of their families. He wrote of a woman whose eighteen-year-old boy had been recently killed in a shooting accident. "I tried to comfort her with pastoral words. I looked at her, standing there tall, in black, her family around her, a family circle. She said to me, 'Father, don't be so sad. Thank you for celebrating with us. It was wonderful. But don't you know that God loves us all. We are mourning, yes, but we know that God is with us.' "

As a priest he went there to make God real to poor people. When he arrived he found that God was already there.

This is Advent. This is the season of preparation for Christmas. So we turn to John the Baptizer to listen to him, because John knows Jesus better than anybody else. John and Jesus were cousins.

John says, "You want to prepare for his coming? I will give you a clue. He stands among you as one you do not know. So expect him to be anywhere: In the stranger, in the friend, among the poor that you go to in his name."

If God can come to us in a manger, he can show up anywhere. So be prepared.

Now for Something Completely Different

Advent 4   **Luke 1:26-38**

If you watch Monty Python on television, you recognize the source for the title of this sermon, "Now for Something Completely Different." For the rest of you, you benighted ones, Monty Python was a troupe of nutty British comedians who performed outrageous skits, highly satirical and often irreverent.

Using Monty Python to introduce a Christmas sermon might seem odd, leading you to wonder whether the old boy has finally gone over the edge. Actually I am more indebted to the novelist Frederick Buechner than I am to Monty Python. Buechner pointed out that the Bible uses comedy to tell the story of God's action in this world.

Comedy is about surprises. Comedy is about the totally different, the impossible ending to a story. The essence of comedy has been analyzed as "irony." Irony describes an event in which what happens is the opposite of what was intended or expected, as when somebody intolerably pompous walks down the street and slips on a banana peel. Or when somebody who is clumsy and slow, like a tortoise wins the

31

race against the hare. Or when the underdog wins the game through a series of incredible circumstances that nobody could believe would ever happen, but they happen, and when they do, everybody laughs for joy. That is irony.

It happens all the time in the Bible. In fact, you could say that the Bible reveals that God rules history in irony. Look at the history of the Jewish people. An outcast people, despised among all the nations, with no land of their own, and yet they, of all people, become the "chosen" people and are given a "promised land."

They get into unbelievable predicaments on their way to possess the land, threatening to forfeit the promise. Eventually they are trapped in slavery in Egypt, but get out of it miraculously. Then a man who can't make a speech is chosen as their leader. Their greatest king starts out as a shepherd boy, the youngest son, the one nobody pays any attention to, but who, virtually unarmed, defeats a giant.

And get this, the whole business begins when a man who is 100 years old and a woman who is over ninety have a baby. You're supposed to laugh at that. History goes from irony to irony. What couldn't possibly happen, happens. It's like one of those old-time movies with Charlie Chaplin or Buster Keaton. The story opens with Abraham and Sarah being promised that their descendants are going to inherit the earth, their children are going to be as numerous as the stars. Years later, they are still childless when an angel visits Abraham and renews the promise, whereupon Abraham falls upon the ground and laughs. What was a beautiful dream is now a bad joke. There is no way that they could have a baby now. It's too late. They are too old.

Then one more visitation. Abraham and Sarah are now ancient. There is no way they could have a baby now. Three angels come to visit them, dressed *incognito* as nomads. Abraham, a good host, invites them to stay for dinner. He tells Sarah, "Go into the kitchen and get the supper ready." She leaves the door open a crack so she can listen, and hears the angel say to Abraham, "Sarah's going to have a baby." This time, it is Sarah who laughs. The angel, hearing Sarah laugh, says, "Is anything too hard for the Lord?" Sarah, embarrassed, stops laughing. The angel, continues, "In the spring I will return and Sarah will have a baby." And he did, and she did. As Genesis put it, "The Lord did to Sarah what he promised."

The point of the Abraham and Sarah story is that God always keeps his promises. You can trust God. "The Lord did to Sarah as he promised." Maybe God doesn't keep his promises when we expect it, but God keeps it. God keeps his promises not according to our time, but according to God's time.

Luke will tell the same story in the first chapter of his gospel, the story of the birth of John the Baptizer. You notice that John the Baptizer's parents, Zechariah and Elizabeth, are old, just like Sarah and Abraham. Luke describes it in these words, "In the days of Herod, King of Judea, there was a priest named Zechariah . . . who had a wife . . . named Elizabeth. And they were both righteous before God . . . But they had no children because Elizabeth was barren, and both were advanced in years."

You see, it's just like Abraham and Sarah. Whenever you hear "both were advanced in years," get ready for some angel to show up with the announcement, "You're going to have a baby." And sure enough, an angel shows up. Old Zechariah, the priest, is at work at the Temple in Jerusalem, kneeling before the altar, doing what priests do. He senses something, the way you get a feeling that somebody is looking at you. He opens one eye and sees the angel standing there at the side of the altar. The angel says, "Don't be afraid, Zechariah. Your prayers have been answered. Elizabeth is going to have a baby, and you shall call his name John."

You Haven't Seen Anything Yet

You see, just like Abraham and Sarah, and several others, incidentally — as in the birth stories of Samson and Samuel — two old folks trying to have a baby, giving up trying, say it's too late, and the angel comes and says, "You're going to have a baby anyway." It's crazy. It's wonderful. It's ironic. What happens is what nobody ever expected would happen.

There are times when life is like a tragedy. The book of Job, Good Friday, and other parts of the Bible describe that honestly. But there are other times when life is like a comedy, when the end is such a wonderful surprise that you laugh for joy. The good guys win after all. Cinderella gets the prince. The victims become the victors. The old couple has a baby.

To believe in God means that you are not surprised when such things happen. It's amazing that they happen, but you're not surprised. Because to believe in God means that you believe God keeps his promise, not in your time but in his time.

That's the point of all of those Annunciation stories to old people in the Bible. It means that sometimes, after we have waited so long that we have given up, so long that we went home, forgot all about it, because it's obviously not going to happen, then it happens, like a miracle. We waited so long there is no way that God is going to keep his promise. Then God keeps it, and everybody laughs for joy.

That happens enough times in the Bible to constitute a pattern, and Luke uses that pattern here in the first chapter of his gospel to tell the story of John the Baptizer. But I warn you that Luke is setting you up. Luke has a mischievous grin on his face as he writes the first chapter. He is setting you up. He wants you to think that because John the Baptizer's birth is just like all these other births described in the Bible, that you can expect the same thing in the birth of Jesus.

But I tell you this. Not many people know this. Luke wanted to put at the top of the second chapter in bold caps, AND NOW FOR SOMETHING COMPLETELY

DIFERENT, but his editor made him take it out. I'm sure that he wanted to put it there. Just look at the second chapter.

It begins with an angel visiting a woman, which ought to get a laugh right-off. Already the unexpected has happened. Angels don't visit women. Everybody knows that. The angel came to Abraham, not to Sarah. The angel came to Zechariah, not to Elizabeth. Even Matthew knew that. According to Matthew, the angel came to Joseph, not to Mary. But here's Luke with something completely different, chuckling as he writes it. The scene opens with the angel visiting Mary, not Joseph.

And what's more, Mary is not old. She is a virgin, which description is used here to point more to her age than to her sexual status. It is not until later that the church becomes more interested in her sexual purity. Right now what Luke is interested in is her age. Mary is just a girl, an adolescent. Mary is young compared to Elizabeth, who was "advanced in years."

Of course, the angel makes the same announcement he always makes. The angel has been making this announcement in the Bible for 1000 years before Mary. He's done it so many times that he's got it memorized. "Hail, O favored one. The Lord is with you. Do not be afraid. You have found favor with God." Then he waits for her response. The response is always the same. The angel has heard it before. "How can this be?" Only this time there is irony. Sarah says, "How can this be? I am too old." But Mary says, "How can this be? I am so young. I have no husband." The angel responds with his prepared reply. "Nothing is impossible" — the same thing he said to Sarah.

So you see, it's the same. Only with an ironic twist. So it's different. It's different enough to get a laugh. God has done it again. God has acted once again, only it's different. To a peasant this time, not to a patriarch or to a priest. To a woman this time, not to a man. To a virgin this time, not to an old woman. Something new and different, something God has never tried before.

We already know that God keeps his promises when God wills, and not when we want. That's what all those other stories reveal. But the story of Mary says, God keeps his promises in ways that we would never expect. Not only will God act any time, but God will act any place, and through anyone . . . even Mary.

So don't ever say that this is the wrong time, or the wrong place, or the wrong person. God loves it when the world sets things up that way and says, "It's never going to happen. It can't happen here. It has never happened that way here before. It can't happen." It's then that God just can't resist pulling the rug out from under us, or placing a banana peel in our path. As Mary sang in the "Magnificat," the song that comes toward the end of this chapter, "He knocks the mighty from their thrones, and exalts them of low degree."

God loves irony. God loves to make happen what we say will never happen. God loves irony because we are so stubborn, narrow-minded, near-sighted, mean-spirited, dull-witted, and unimaginative. He just loves to trip up that kind of people, show us that things can happen that we say will never happen. Things happen all the time that people said will never happen. Have you ever said, "What will they think of next?" You usually say that in relation to technology. There doesn't seem to be anything that technology can't do, "What will they think of next?" Well, God loves to confound some dull-witted rationalist and really astound him, or shake up her world, in the hope that they will say, "What will God think of next?"

That could be the reason why he made Christmas, so that one of these years you will stumble over it, pick yourself up and ask, "What does Christmas really mean?" and be absolutely astounded. Christmas ought to leave you laughing for joy, delighting in it all, the irony of it all. Christmas ought to leave you walking down the road toward the new year shaking your head saying, "What will God think of next?"

Milan Kundera is a Czech writer, now living in exile in Paris because his writings offended the communist government of Czechoslovakia. They wanted to get rid of him. It is significant that Kundera is known as a writer of comedy. He writes about the irony of history. One of his books is entitled *Forgetting and Laughter* in which he pokes fun at governments that take themselves too seriously, which means all governments. He writes this wonderful paragraph.

> *We are all prisoners of a rigid conception of what is important and what is not. We anxiously follow what we suppose to be important, while what we suppose to be unimportant wages guerrilla warfare behind our backs transforming the world without our knowledge.*

That's an ironic view of history. It is thoroughly biblical, and describes Christmas perfectly. In those days they thought Rome was what was important, while what they thought was unimportant was quietly transforming the world behind their backs.

That ought to encourage you. If you are praying for peace in this world, if you are working to end the nuclear madness, then that perspective ought to give you hope. If you are working for justice in this world, if you are working to free all people from tyranny, or if you are working for compassion for the hungry, or the homeless, then Christmas ought to give you reason to keep on working.

Or if you are just struggling with your own problems, if the systems of this world, even those relatively insignificant ones that impinge upon your life, have become oppressive to you, or if you are fighting a battle against some bondage, if there is some enemy inside of you, or if you fear that you are not worth very much; or if you worry that your children are not going to amount to anything, then the story of Christmas is for you.

Christmas says that behind what we consider the important facts, God is working, transforming the world without our knowledge, quietly working, according to his timetable, not ours, and in ways that he chooses, not in ways that we would ever expect — just as he did 2000 years ago when he sent an angel to Mary, just a girl, nobody would have guessed it, and said, "Hail, O favored one." The Lord is with you."

A Momentous Trifle

Christmas Eve/Day   *Luke 2:1-20*

In some newly declassified documents from the State Department, there's a paragraph from the minutes of the National Security Council dated September 12, 1954. It reads like this, "Secretary Dulles said that in Japan he had a lengthy meeting with Premier Yoshida. Secretary Dulles told Yoshida frankly that Japan should not expect to find a big U.S. market, because the Japanese don't make things that Americans want."

They did something about that.

There are a number of lessons there, but the one I want to point out is that there is a history invisible to those who see only what is on the main stage. Not many people bother to investigate what's behind the scenes. We assume that what is on stage now is what is really important, especially if it is big and powerful, as the United States was in 1954. Virtually unchallenged militarily and industrially, it was center stage in the world, in the limelight. As a symbol of that status the American automotive industry built big and powerful cars which were to be labeled "insolent chariots."

39

Nobody noticed in 1954 what was going on in the wings, backstage. In the Far East, an incipient industrial base that would one day humble the American automotive industry was being put together. In the Middle East, where the oil needed to run the big and powerful cars came from, there were the first rumblings of a renewed Islamic nationalism. In 1954, nobody paid attention to those things. They were happening behind the scenes, backstage.

There was another reason why we paid no attention. We believed that what we did in America would affect the rest of the world, not the other way around. The rest of the world was made up of "dependent nations." We never thought that what would happen in a tiny defeated nation or in a medieval desert kingdom would ever affect us.

I suppose the way the world was in 1954 was similar to the way it was in the First Century. Rome was a huge power with dependent nations. All nations in the Mediterranean world were dependent upon Rome. We have records from that period, official records, dispatches from the provinces, from the consulates, reporting on what was going on in the Empire. They make no mention of the birth of a baby named Jesus to a peasant family named Mary and Joseph in a little town named Bethlehem in a province named Judea. Not a word. You can't find any record of it anywhere in any official document.

But here it is in Luke. It's in Luke because Luke is writing a behind-the-scenes history of the First Century. Luke says that's where God works, behind the scenes, in the wings, in what Edmund Burke called "the trifles of history," the events and the people that nobody pays attention to because they're not on stage. They're not in the limelight. They're in the wings. So nobody pays attention to them.

Luke has a particular bias about history. Every historian does. Everybody has a point of view. Luke sees history from the perspective of the forgotten, the downtrodden and the woebegone. The Bible calls those people the *anawim*, which translates, "the poor ones," the people whom nobody pays attention to. But Luke says you'd better pay attention to them, because, and this is Luke's bias, when God acted in history, God acted through them. When God took on human flesh, he took on poor flesh. Luke doesn't want us to forget that, so he writes history from that perspective, from behind the scenes, and therefore with a certain irony, revealing that things are not always as they seem.

Luke begins where you have to begin if you're writing a history of the First Century; he begins with Rome, the most dominating power in the history of the whole world. You've got to begin with Rome. He says, "In those days a decree went out from Caesar Augustus." When that happens, the whole world takes notice; even small Judea, thousands of miles away, takes notice when Rome roars.

But Luke, who begins reporting what is on the stage, moves immediately backstage. From behind the scenes he reports that there was another announcement, this one given at the same time, in the same year, but this one not from Caesar; this one is from God, and not to the whole world, but to shepherds. "And the angel of the Lord appeared to them, and the glory of the Lord shone round about them."

Here's the irony. When Rome speaks, the whole world hears it. When God speaks, it's always a whisper. That Roman census was especially onerous to the Jews. In fact, any census was met with resistance by the Jews. They still remembered with bitterness the one that old King David tried to put over on them hundreds of years before. Any mention of that Davidic census made them angry. This one, the Roman census, would galvanize a resistance into a political movement called the Zealot party, which eventually would wage a guerrilla warfare against Rome and cause Rome to come down to destroy the city. That was in A.D. 70.

41

So the census is bad news. The year of the census is a
date that would live in infamy. In that year, the bad year,
the year of the bad news from Caesar Augustus, an angel
appeared to the shepherds saying, "Behold I bring you good
news that has come to all people."

Luke wants you to ponder that. On the main stage, same
old bad news, same old oppressor, same violent reaction to
it. In the wings, good news to all people, a savior with a whole
new way of living in this world.

And it came to shepherds. Luke makes much of that. Our
image of shepherds has been shaped by Sunday school
pageants, little boys in bathrobes, a little unruly at times,
but it adds to the quaintness of the scene. It's all very innocent. That has shaped our vision of shepherds.

But the real ones were not that way at all. They were
not innocent. They were known, as a class, to be dishonest,
unprincipled hustlers and cheaters. Some of them were out-
laws. Richard Avedon, the famous fashion photographer, published a book of photographs of western faces. He traveled
in Montana, Colorado, Texas, and some other states and took
pictures of people who worked on the ranches and in the small
towns. It's the kind of book you get for Christmas, a big ex-
pensive book that you put on the coffee table. If you've seen
those pictures, then you've seen the kind of people who would
have been shepherds: the underclass, the poor, drifters, dis-
franchised, unattractive, unlikely hosts for visiting angels.

It's no accident that Luke puts those people there.
Shepherds are not there in Luke's gospel to provide a quaint,
pastoral touch to an enchanting scene. The shepherds are
there to make the point that when God acts in this world,
he acts through the *anawim,* the poor ones, the ones who are
in the wings permanently unnoticed.

In those days, when Caesar Augustus sent his imperial
decree carried by soldiers to the ends of the world, God sent
his heavenly decree carried by angels to outcasts. They're the

ones who tell Mary the meaning of what has happened to
her. She hears about it through the poor ones, the *anawim*,
the outcasts, and ponders what they said in her heart.

That's as far as it goes. No headlines, no distinguished
visitors. It's Matthew who has the wise men come, not Luke.
Luke says, "There were only shepherds there," whose reputation must have caused Mary to have some fright when they
walked through the stable door in the middle of the night.
She recognized who they were, but they did her no harm.
Instead they told her what they had seen and heard, left, and
told no one, or maybe, because of who they were, no one
paid any attention. And Mary said nothing, just pondered
it, out of sight, off-camera, behind the scenes, just a trifle
of history. But it changed the world.

In the year of bad news, there came Good News. That's
what Luke would have us ponder.

And this. During the time of the mighty Caesars God
came as a helpless babe. To appreciate what Luke does with
this, you have to remember something about Caesar Augustus. In the first place, he has a month named after him.
That's for openers. His name has also become an adjective
for a prosperous and enlightened age. An "augustan age"
is an age of high civilization. It's a rare privilege to live in
an augustan age. But even more significantly, for Luke's pur-
poses, Caesar Augustus was known as the ruler who had
brought peace to the world. That's what he was known for.
That's what all the fuss over Caesar Augustus was about.
There is even today in Rome a statue in honor of Caesar Augustus, the peacemaker, because it was Caesar Augustus who
brought an end to the internecine wars that threatened to
destroy the Empire. Caesar Augustus was known in those
days as the "Prince of Peace." There were statues and
shrines in his honor in all the provinces of the empire. One
of them has the inscription, "Caesar Augustus, Savior of the
Whole World."

Caesar Augustus is on main stage, that's true. But he's just a warm-up act. The real Messiah is getting ready to make his appearance.

Luke has a particular bias. You can see this throughout all of his gospel. He sees history from the point of view of the forgotten, the downtrodden, and the woebegone, the ones the Bible calls the *anawim,* the poor ones. The ones that Jesus said would always be with us. The ones that no one pays any attention to. But Luke says you better pay attention to them because when God acted to save the world, he did it through them. Luke wants us to ponder that.

I lift up three things to ponder.

1. God is in charge. The Christmas story is about that. We think the Christmas story is about Mary and Joseph and a baby. But it isn't, not really. They are just there as the actors. Luke says that the director of this drama is God, and that everyone else is an actor. Augustus Caesar is an actor. Tiberius, Quirinius, John the Baptizer, Mary, Joseph, even Jesus, are actors. The director is God. God is in charge. What we do at Christmas, therefore, is to celebrate what God has done, and ponder what it means for us. Could it mean that God is working in our world the way he did then? Could it mean that God is working in my life the way he did in theirs?

Frederick Buechner says you ought to listen to your life. "Listen to the boredom and the pain, as well as the excitement and the gladness." Because if God works the way that Luke says God does, then all moments of your life are potentially significant moments. All areas of your life are places where epiphanies can happen. At any time, even in the year of bad news, good news may come from unlikely messengers. If God is the director, then maybe we ought to listen for his direction.

2. *God likes happy endings.* The purpose of God's direction is to have good come out of your life, and to have the Kingdom of God come on earth. That's what Christmas says. And God is at work in this world to make sure that that happens.

The reason that Luke uses so much Old Testament prophesy in talking about the birth of Jesus — the first two chapters of Luke are filled with Old Testament prophesy — is to show that God keeps his promises. You can trust God. God is faithful.

That ought to give us a certain equanimity in this life, an ability to take what happens in stride, in confidence that good is going to come out of it because God is in charge of it.

Luke also wrote the Book of Acts. The Book of Acts is a history of the early church, the history of the first Christians. William Willimon wrote of the Book of Acts, "If you read it, you get the feeling that you are in the presence of people who have the quiet confidence that they are in the winning camp." That's what ought to characterize Christians, a quiet confidence that God is in charge, and therefore, somehow, there will be a happy ending.

3. *And finally, we will never be able to forget the poor or to take lightly their cry for justice in this world, not since Christmas.* Some believe that Luke is writing his gospel to a well-heeled, well-educated, well-established congregation that has forgotten its humble beginnings. That's why he emphasizes Jesus' teachings about being humble. The teachings about humility are not there to keep the humble in their place. They are there for the proud, the strong, the wealthy, not to take their place too seriously, or to think that they are where they are because God thinks they are such wonderful people. They are where they are for all kinds of reasons, not one of which can be attributed to divine favor. That ought to make them humble, and wary. Because if God favors anyone in this world, according to Luke, it's not the powerful, it's the weak; it's not the rich, it's the poor.

The lesson the rich and the powerful should learn from all this is humility. Humility means to care for other people the way that God has cared for us, to use some of the wealth we have accumulated that makes our lives comfortable to help someone else live decently. Humility means that you had better remember your humanity. Not even Caesar is God. We are all in the same boat, all in the same family, and we should live that way.

Remember the least of these — that's the message from Christmas, from Luke's point of view. And he won't let you miss that, not if you read him carefully. Luke says, "When God came into this world, he came not to the powerful. He came to the weak. He came to an illiterate girl in a bruised world in a dark time and said, 'Blessed are you among all women on earth.' " And when she gave birth it was in a town that she didn't want to be in, but she was the kind that gets pushed around. She wanted to be home, but she gave birth in a town in which she was a stranger, one of the *anawim*. The shepherds came, startling her, because she was just a girl and they were rough men. But instead of harming her, they told her that they had seen a vision and heard angel voices saying that the one whom everyone is waiting for has come, and he will bring peace to this world and good will among all people. "Do you think," they asked, "your baby is the one?"

She listened to them and thanked them. Then they left, and she pondered all of this in her heart . . . and wept for fear and for joy. God, who directs the drama of history, had arranged a happy ending, not just for her, but for the whole world.

Why Can't Christmas Last Forever?

Christmas 1   **Luke 2:22-40**

There is a marvelous story at the end of the second chapter of Luke to be read on the First Sunday after Christmas. It is the story of Simeon. It is perfect for Christmas, and for the last Sunday of the year.

The scene is an old man holding a baby. Can't you just see that? Perhaps you did see it over the holidays. The grandparents, or maybe the great-grandparents, came for Christmas. They wanted to be there especially this Christmas because the new baby was going to be there. Mary, or whatever her name is, had her baby, so they would be there. It would be a special Christmas. It always is with a new baby.

The grandparents brought a little gift, something the baby will have to grow into, of course, something practical — the kind of thing that grandparents give. Mary hands the baby to her grandfather, the baby's great-grandfather. He can hardly see anymore, his gnarled hands holding this new life, his wrinkled old face looking down into innocence.

That's a beautiful image, an old man and a baby. It's the image that Luke draws of Simeon and the baby Jesus at the end of the second chapter of Luke. Why is it there?

47

You Haven't Seen Anything Yet

The text says that Mary and Joseph were careful to observe all of the Jewish laws concerning the birth of babies, so on the eighth day they took the baby to the Temple for the circumcision, just as the law required. Then they went back to Bethlehem to wait four weeks for another ritual, the ritual of purification of a mother after a birth.

The time comes to go to the Temple. The month of waiting is over. They are all packed. They got the donkey loaded, a little yellow sign on the back of the donkey, "Baby On Board." They are going to tend to the Ritual of Purification.

The text says they made an offering of turtledoves for the purification. The standard offering was a lamb, but the law allowed the giving of turtledoves if you were poor. Luke put that little detail in there as another subtle reminder that Jesus identified with the poor, so much so that he was born into poor folks' home. Mary and Joseph couldn't afford a lamb. They could only afford two turtledoves.

As they walk up the steps to the Temple, an old man confronts them, asks to see the baby. This is the way Luke describes it. "There was a man in Jerusalem, whose name was Simeon, and this man was righteous and devout, looking for the consolation of Israel."

Which means he was looking for the Messiah. That's why he's there. He was probably stationed at the Temple because of that prophesy in the Book of Malachi that said when the Messiah comes he will "suddenly come to his Temple." So Simeon stands there at the top of the steps at the Temple looking for the Messiah, waiting for him to come to his Temple. He has been there for years, checking out the babies, seeing if this is the one that we are waiting for. Is this the one what is the consolation of Israel? Year after year after year he had been there, checking out the babies.

The Old Testament lesson for this Sunday from Isaiah reveals that prophets had two functions in Israel. They were spokespersons for God. You saw in this same passage that

Anna is also a prophet and was there in the temple. Prophets were spokespersons for God. But prophets were also intercessors for the people. Not only did they tell the people what God wanted them to hear; they also told God what the people wanted God to hear, which was mostly complaints, such as, "When are you going to send the Messiah that you promised?" Isaiah said, "For Zion's sake I will not keep silent, and for Jerusalem's sake I will not rest." Isaiah saw himself as an advocate, as a lobbyist for the people in the courts of the Almighty, pleading the case of the people before God.

Simeon evidently saw himself as an advocate prophet, too, because he is there in the temple reminding God of his promise. He stands there at the top of the steps the way a watchman stands on the wall scanning the horizon looking for "the consolation of Israel."

He sees Mary, Joseph, and the baby coming up the steps. Picture Simeon there at the top of the steps, arms outstretched crying, "Let me see the baby!" You can imagine what Mary thought. "He's crazy, this old man. He'll probably drop him." Reluctantly, Mary gives him the child. Simeon pulls down the cover of the little blanket, looks into the baby's face, and sings: "Lord, now lettest Thou Thy servant depart in peace, according to Thy word; for mine eyes have seen Thy salvation."

The Messiah has come! The Savior of the World is here! That's the way Luke concludes his Christmas story. He draws the image of an old man holding a baby, announcing: "This is he! This is the one that we've been waiting for. The Messiah is come! The consolation of Israel is here!"

Why does he do that? Why does he have to make that announcement at the end of the Christmas story? Some say that Simeon represents Israel, old Israel, waiting all these years for the coming of the Messiah. Old Israel is superceded now, the way a new year, symbolized by a baby, supercedes the old year, symbolized by Father Time, the old man.

That may be what Luke had in mind, but it didn't work out that way historically. Israel was not superceded. Israel is still around. Israel is still waiting, as a matter of fact, for the Messiah. And Christianity hasn't exactly taken over politically, since there are still a lot of non-Christian nations around, and even the so-called Christian nations aren't very Christian. So the scene is not the image of Messianic triumph, triumph of the new over the old.

I see this: Luke has to announce that the Messiah has come. And he has somebody do it who knows what he is looking for, because it wasn't obvious that the Messiah had come. How many people saw it? The day after Jesus was born, the sun rose as usual to reveal the usual; the Romans were still occupying the land. The Jews were still under occupation. That onerous census continued to crank out its bureaucratic trouble for everybody. Society didn't change. The rich continued to be rich. The sick continued to be sick. The problems that plagued humankind didn't disappear. Not when the Messiah came.

Luke must have heard all of these questions, these reservations. "If the Messiah has come he certainly got past me. I must have missed it. Are you sure he came? The world continues to be messed up. My life continues to have all of its nagging problems. Are you sure he came?"

On Christmas day, on Christmas Eve especially, it is different. Then it is wonderful. Everybody is nice to each other, at least making the effort, even brothers and sisters for a while, making the effort. On Christmas Day the newspapers report some really magnificent efforts at helping people who have problems in this world. It's the best day to read the newspaper because of the moving stories of people feeding the hungry, housing the homeless. The network news on the holy day ends the program with some sentimental vignette about people loving one another. We seem to be able to get it all together for twenty-four hours, but that's about all. The next day the news returns to normal.

Several years ago I read a column by Mike Royko, the Chicago newspaper columnist, published the day after Christmas. He wrote it to remind us that Christmas doesn't last forever. He told about a man driving home on Christmas Eve who saw a boy fall through the ice on a lagoon. The man stopped his car, jumped out, took his coat off, laid it on the bank, and crawled out on the ice to save the boy. The ice broke and the man fell in, but he was still able to rescue the boy, risking his own life to do so. It's a wonderful story for Christmas; a man reaching out to help somebody else, risking his own life.

Shivering and shaking, the man climbed out of the water, picked up his coat from the ground, and discovered that while he had been risking his life, somebody had been lifting his wallet.

Royko didn't stop there. He told other sentiment-bashing stories, such as the department store Santa Claus who, instead of putting a pillow in his costume, stuffed it with merchandise from the store. They arrested him, searched his house, found his basement was filled with stolen merchandise. He was running his own department store out of the basement, a Chicago version of Santa's workshop.

I really resent reading that stuff. I want to believe that there is something permanent about the spirit of Christmas, that it can change people. In fact, I want to believe that the spirit of Christmas can change the world. I want Tiny Tim to be happy, and I want Scrooge to be kind. I want Christmas to change things.

There are truces at Christmas time, at least if it is Christians killing one another. That happened most recently during the civil wars in Nicaragua and El Salvador. The one in Nicaragua didn't work, but the one in El Salvador did. They didn't kill anybody for twenty-four hours.

I wondered about this. If we can stop fighting for one day, why couldn't it go on for the second day, and then for

51

the day after that? Couldn't those people who are hooked on war stop, the way the other addicts with life-threatening habits stop — one day at a time? Why can't that happen?

I guess it just isn't that kind of world; not yet. It's still the kind of world where that hope is seen to be naive and simplistic.

So, has the Messiah really come? It's the same question as, "Why can't Christmas last all year?" If you have ever hoped that the Christmas spirit would last forever, that it would transform the world permanently, then you have an idea of what Israel was waiting for. They were waiting for the transformation of this world into the Kingdom of God. They believed the transformation of the world would happen first, then the Messiah would come. First, everything would be changed, which meant there would be no mistaking his coming. You would know the time, because everything would be changed. It would be obvious when the Messiah came, no mistaking it.

But it wasn't that way, not at all. That's why after Luke tells the story, the annunciations to Mary and to Elizabeth, the visitation of the shepherds, the nativity scene, all the beautiful stories, Luke has to end the story with the announcement: "This baby really is the Messiah! This really is the one you are looking for! I know it doesn't look like it. I know nothing has changed. But look at this. Here is an old man, Simeon. He's been looking for the Messiah all these years. He is a respected old man. He's a prophet. He's an expert in looking for the Messiah. He holds the baby, and says, 'This is it.' " Then he sings that beautiful song we call the "Nunc Dimittis," because in Latin the first two words of the song are *Nunc dimittis*. "Lord, now lettest Thou Thy servant depart in peace, according to Thy word; for mine eyes have seen Thy salvation."

An old man and a baby. The old man, an advocate for the people, asking God, "When are you going to keep your promise? When are you going to send the one who will save the people? When are you going to redeem this world?" That's the man who said, "This is the one. The Messiah is come. God has acted." Old Simeon ought to know because he has made a career out of waiting for the Messiah.

The old man says something more. You've got to read on in the text, which we seldom do. The "Nunc Dimittis" does not end with "Lord let Thy servant depart in peace for mine eyes have seen Thy salvation." It ends with "This child is set for the fall and rising of many in Israel . . . and a sword will pierce through your own soul also." That last word is for Mary. "A sword shall pierce your soul as well." That refers to the time when her son will grow up, be arrested, tortured, crucified, and die. Perhaps it also refers to that moment in her life when he will go on his own, even rebuke her. That must have pierced her soul as well.

But the other word is for us. "This child is set for the fall and the rising of many." In the Bible when a prophet sets something "before the people," it means that it's now up to the people. The people have to make a choice now. The prophets had a way of doing that. They brought things home to the people by asking, "Now what do you think of this? Which path are you going to take? What decision are you going to make?"

Luke, like a prophet, has set Christmas before us the same way. He's finished telling the story, a beautiful story. He just sets it there before us. It's not a panacea for our problems. It's not a magic kingdom. It's not a supernaturally imposed order from above. It's not something that is done for us at all. It's something that challenges us to do something. This child is set before us now. What are we going to do with him?

He's not going to solve the problems that you wrestle with, but you can, by following him. He's not going to take away the pain that you suffer, but you can bear that pain redemptively, by following him. He's not going to end the fighting in this world, but you can, by following him.

An old man and a baby. Just look at him. He stares at that baby. He wants to be sure. He's been waiting for this so long; he doesn't want to make a mistake now. He looks at the baby for the longest time. A smile comes over his face. It's the wonderful smile of an old man. You know that smile, the kind that shines through years of hard work under the sun, back-breaking work, the years of disappointment and sadness. They were written there on that face. Then the smile, the kind that you can see only on the face of an old person. The smile of joy. The tears filling the old eyes. "Lord, now let Thy servant depart in peace. I'm ready to go now. For mine eyes have seen Thy salvation."

But stay with him; old Simeon is not finished with his song. "This child is set for the fall and rising of many." You know what Simeon does when he sings that line? He hands the baby to you and says, "Here, hold him. Look at him."

You see, Simeon has made his choice. "Mine eyes have seen Thy salvation." Then he hands the baby to you. That's why Simeon is there at the end of the second chapter of Luke. He is there to end the Christmas story by handing the baby to you, asking, "Now what do you see?"

The Story Behind the News

The assassination of President Kennedy continues to hold the attention of the nation. Books are still being published asking, how did it happen? Who did it? What did it mean?

A few years ago there was a novel written entitled *Promises to Keep.* The supposition was, what if Kennedy survived that assassination and was still living? What would the world be like?

The author, a man named Bernau, received the largest advance ever for a first-time novelist, $750,000. When the book was published he was interviewed around the country and even in Great Britain.

More than twenty-five years have passed since the death of Kennedy, and the questions have not gone away. In fact, they are probably approached more seriously now, because the perspective of twenty-five years gives us a more careful assessment of what happened and what it means.

Besides that, a whole new generation, born since 1963, is coming into adulthood and asking questions. They were not alive when it happened, or were just babies. They know nothing of the enormous impact Kennedy's assassination had on the lives of so many people, his disciples, those who were devoted to him, especially, but also on many others all around the world who hoped that he might be the one who would lead this nation into a new era of greatness. They weren't so much passionate followers as those who stood back and waited to see if the promise would be fulfilled.

One day in Dallas it all came to an end. But after twenty-five years the questions are still being asked, the books still being written.

It occurred to me that the first books written about Jesus appeared almost exactly twenty-five years after his Crucifixion and Resurrection. Those books ask the same questions: Who did it? Why did it happen? And especially, what does it mean for us?

Look at the Gospel of Mark, the first gospel written. You could say that the Gospel of Mark is really a commentary on the Crucifixion, what happened and what it means. Mark was written almost exactly twenty-five years after the Crucifixion and Resurrection.

The other gospels came on Mark's heels: Matthew, Luke, and John. And there were other gospels that didn't get into the New Testament, some of which have been found, such as the "Gospel of Thomas." So we know that a generation after Jesus' Crucifixion and Resurrection, twenty-five years later, a spate of books was published to answer the questions: What happened? What does it mean?

There were also some sensational writings about the event. We'd call them novels, speculations about what happened to Jesus. They assume that he did not die but somehow escaped and is now living it up in Egypt or some other place. Those were not serious books. The gospels were serious books, attempting to explain what happened, who was this Jesus, what does he mean for us?

Twenty-five years after the event there was a new generation, raised in the church, but born after the Resurrection. The gospels probably were written for them, those who, in the words of John, "believe but didn't see." This generation was like Thomas in the Gospel of John; they weren't there when Jesus appeared in the Resurrection, so they had questions. The Gospels were written to answer the questions they raised. That's what a gospel is for. A gospel is there to tell the whole story, to tell what happened and what it means for us.

Mark, the first of the gospels, was written around A.D. 55. John, the last of the four gospels, and perhaps the most sophisticated, was written around A.D. 90-95. It's John that we're going to look at this Sunday in Christmastide.

John's purpose was the same as the other three gospels, to tell the story of Jesus and to explain what it means for us, but he has a unique way of doing this. You can see that in his version of the story of Christmas.

The setting, according to John, is not the little town of Bethlehem. The setting for Christmas is the whole universe. Christmas was not an isolated event in a remote village. It was a cosmic event that inaugurated a new era in the history of the world. Jesus may have been a helpless baby lying in a manger, whose life was threatened by the jealousy of a tyrannical king. But that's not the real story. That's not the story behind the news. The story behind the news, what really happened, is this: God decided that now is the time that he would redeem the world, and so he acted to do it. Once God decided to redeem the world, nothing could stop him; not Herod the Great, who was the king at Jesus' birth, or Herod Antipas, who was the king at Jesus' Crucifixion, or Pilate, or Caesar, or anything else could stop God from doing what God wanted to do, which was to redeem the world. Christmas, according to John, is like an invasion force whose victory is assured the moment it lands.

And the wonderful irony of it all is that God did it through a baby, not an army. God is going to redeem the world through love, not through force. God came here in the form of a baby because we got here in the form of babies, and God is going to show his love for us by becoming one of us. The way the Bible talks about that is to say that God sent his Son, or as John puts it, "his only begotten Son." But what it really means is that God himself is with us.

That's the story John tells in a uniquely beautiful way in this first chapter. In the Greek the text reads more like poetry than prose. It's ingenious the way he picks up images out of the Greek and Hebrew cultures and weaves them together to tell this Christmas story. John was obviously writing for both Jews and Greeks, so you've got to listen out of both your Jewish and your Greek ears at the same time.

He says that if you think that the story of Christmas began at Bethlehem, you're mistaken. Christmas began in the Creation. The first words of John's Gospel are the same words that begin the Book of Genesis, "In the beginning . . ."

"In the beginning was the Word . . ." The Greeks personified that idea of "the Word," so you've got to let yourself go and think Greek for a minute. Think of the Word as a person. "The Word" was like an architect or an engineer, a builder or a foreman. The Word is what built the world, so the Word knows what God's plan for everything is, the way things are supposed to be.

The Jews had a similar idea called "Wisdom" which was also personified and functioned as sort of an architect of the world. If you want to read about Wisdom read what is called the wisdom literature such as Proverbs in the Old Testament. If your Bible has an Apocrypha, then read the Book of Ecclesiasticus. Both are part of the biblical collection of wisdom literature. They say that in the beginning was Wisdom, just as John says that in the beginning was the Word.

Now look at what John does with this:

> *... all things were made through him, and without him was not anything made that was made. In him was life, and the life was the light of men ...*

What an amazing affirmation. Since all things were made through him, and since the Word and God are one, therefore, when you look at Creation you can see God. God is available to everyone. Do you remember the old missionary story out of Africa? Missionaries brought the story of God to a tribe that had never heard God's name before. They listened and then said, "We have known him all along by a different name." "All things are made through him." Therefore, God is available to everybody.

Then this other powerful affirmation:

> *The light shines in the darkness, and the darkness has not overcome it.*

There's a struggle in the world between evil and good. We all know that. In the Gospel of John that is symbolized by light representing good and darkness evil. John says goodness is going to win because goodness is built into the Creation. It's part of the foundation. Evil never stops trying to defeat it, but evil cannot destroy good.

Is that why goodness is so resilient in this world? Is that why no matter what evil does to some people, they become more decent, more noble? Is that why when evil has done its worst, new life always appears? Because "The light shines in the darkness, and the darkness has not overcome it."

I've heard people ask, "Why is there evil in this world?" They could just as well ask, "Why is there good in this world?" There is so much evil in the world, as we have seen in the Twentieth Century, that the greater wonder is that evil doesn't destroy it. But it doesn't. And it doesn't because it cannot. "The light shines in the darkness, and the darkness has not overcome it . . ."

Then skip down to the famous fourteenth verse. This is John's nativity. This is John's story of Christmas. He summarized it in one verse.

> *. . . The Word became flesh and dwelt among us, full of grace and truth . . .*

In the period when Jewish literature was influenced by Greek ideas, there was a legend that said that out of love God sent Wisdom to Israel, and now Wisdom "dwells" in the Torah. That is to say, Wisdom is to be found in the Bible, the Jewish Bible. So if you want to know God, read the Bible.

John knew that legend, so he knows what he's doing when he says, ". . . the Word became flesh and dwelt among us . . ." He is saying that God came to be with us, not in a book, but in a human being. So if you want to know God, if you want to know who God is, if you want to know what God is like, look at Jesus. Because God ". . . became flesh and dwelt among us, full of grace and truth . . ."

And to emphasize that Jesus is God Incarnate, John says:

> *. . . we have beheld his glory, glory as of the only Son from the Father.*

Glory is all you can see of God. Glory is the aura that surrounds God. No one can see God. Looking at God is like looking at the sun. All you can see is the brightness of his glory. So wherever God appears, God is always hidden. But God's glory is there. He can't hide his glory. So, "We have beheld His glory."

Then the passage ends with these words:

> *No one has ever seen God; the only Son, who is in the bosom of the Father, he has made Him known.*

That's what Christmas is, according to John. That's the story behind the news.

There are many levels of meaning in Christmas. I used to get impatient when people would say something that I thought had nothing at all to do with Christmas, then conclude with, "After all, that's what Christmas is all about." The fact is, Christmas is about a lot of things. There are many dimensions to Christmas, from the frivolous to the profound, from the material to the spiritual, from the secular to the holy. They are all there. And we shouldn't be self-righteous about how other people celebrate Christmas. It can be celebrated many ways. What we have in John's gospel is an interpretation of Christmas for that time in your life when you are looking for something deep and profound.

A man was moved by the example of courageous sacrifice of a family in the time of crisis. It got him to thinking about deep things. He got to thinking about religious faith. What does it mean? He pointed out that there were those who do not have religious faith and believe that it is a sign of weakness. They reject what they call "the consolations of religion." This man, whose name is John Garvey, questioned whether belief in Christian faith really is a consolation. It certainly is not when faith means being loyal to the God that demands obedience from us. And neither is there anything consoling in the picture of God who won't answer his Son's prayers when his Son prays that the cup of death might pass from him.

Then he asks, what difference does religious faith make? He answers by saying the difference is in the way you respond to terrible times, which takes him back to the example of that family. They had a child who fell ill while staying with relatives and suffered severe and permanent brain damage. That child needs constant attention now, and the parents give it to him. They have no vacations. They have very little social life. They have lots of reasons to complain and gripe, but they don't. They respond instead only with love.

He wrote:

> *I felt, looking at him and at them, that there are depths here which are holy, and a mystery of love which cannot be spoken about very well. . . .*
>
> *It is the mystery which leads us to baptize infants, which tells us that God's relationship with this person is not as limited as our own. The moment that this realization begins to be marginal among Christians, we will have begun to betray an essential part of what it is that we have been given as a vocation, the work of saying and living as if it were so, that the Creation is holy, that what is good, even when it is terribly wounded, is holy, and maybe especially then.*

He concludes with this quotation from Simone Weil: "Love is not consolation. Love is light."

Wonderful. What he saw in that family was light shining in the darkness, and the darkness could not overcome it. Because love is not mere consolation; love is light that renews and redeems.

That's what John is saying. He is saying, this is hard, hard to put into words. But he tries. He says the light has always been here, since the Creation. And it's everywhere. You can see it in the love of that family. And the darkness has never been able to put it out.

At Christmas we saw that light in its fullness, or at least in all the fullness that we can stand. And it was glorious. It was "glory as of the only Son from the Father."

The Secret Message

The Baptism of Our Lord   *Mark 1:4-11*

The first time you read through the four gospels you probably got the impression that they were all alike, and said, "If you've read one you've read them all." They tell the same story. They tell it much the same way, especially the first three gospels: Matthew, Mark, and Luke. They are so much alike that they are grouped together and called the "synoptic Gospels." "Synoptic" means to see through the same eye.

So, you've read one, you've read them all. No point in reading all of them. Save time by reading one. Pick the smallest one, the Gospel of Mark. Stamp out redundancy! Right?

Wrong! Read them a second time and you will become aware that there are indeed differences among them. The longer you live with them, the more you are aware of subtle differences that make each gospel unique, the way a parent with four children who look so much alike that people are always confusing them knows each child as unique. In fact the parent is amazed that four children raised under the same roof, having the same genes, could be so different.

63

You Haven't Seen Anything Yet

So it is with the gospels. There are differences that you will not notice unless you live with them for a while, or unless someone points them out to you, which I am about to do.

Take the story of the Baptism of Jesus, for example. All three synoptic gospels record it — Matthew, Mark, and Luke — and John alludes to it. So they all mention it. The three who describe it tell essentially the same story. It goes like this:

John the Baptizer is at the River Jordan baptizing the Jews in preparation for the coming of the the Kingdom of God. The purpose of baptism was to get everybody ready. Here comes Jesus down to the river. John baptizes him. The heavens open, and God says, "This is my beloved Son in whom I am well pleased." Jesus comes out of the water, heads out to the desert, and begins his ministry.

That's it. They all say that, but there are differences. The obvious difference is that Luke's version is much longer. You can see that right away. Then in Matthew there is a fascinating detail. According to Matthew, John tries to get out of baptizing Jesus, like someone who sees a better qualified colleague in the audience says, "You should be up here, not me." Matthew records John saying, "I need to be baptized by you." No one but Matthew mentions that interesting detail.

Here's another difference I want to point out to you. I bet you've never noticed this. It has to do with the description of the heavens opening and the voice saying, "This is my beloved son . . ." In Matthew and in Luke it says, "The heavens were opened . . ." But in Mark it says, "He saw the heavens open . . ." Which means that in Matthew and in Luke this decisive event was a public event, but in Mark it was private. In Matthew and Luke the heavens "were opened" and everybody saw it. But according to Mark, only Jesus saw it. "He saw the heavens open." So in Mark, it's a private experience, a personal epiphany, a secret message. Nobody else there saw it.

64

"And when he came out of the water, immediately he saw the heavens open." That's what it says, which is astounding when you notice that the whole nation is at the River Jordan. Mark says that all of Judea "went out to him, and all the people of Jerusalem," which I take to mean everybody. The whole nation was out there, gathered at the River Jordan, awaiting the coming of the Kingdom of God, getting ready for it, John the Baptizer shouting, "Prepare the way of the Lord!" What a marvelous scene this is! He's dunking the whole nation into the River Jordan.

Of course, Mark draws it in such a way as to make his point. So it's not a photograph. It's not an actual historical record of what happened. It's more like a painting, an impressionist painting, to reveal the real meaning under the surface of the event. It's drawn with imagination.

Mark said, "All of the nation is there at the river." Imagine it! A great, giant canvas he's painting, like the Crucifixion at Forest Lawn in Glendale, or the Cyclorama in Atlanta. Everybody there, gathered at the River Jordan, the loud speakers blaring, "Shall we gather at the river . . ."

Their being at the River Jordan is also of tremendous significance. The River Jordan was no ordinary river. It was across the Jordan that they had passed in order to enter the Promised Land a thousand years before. The Jordan was to the Jews what Plymouth Rock is to Americans. It's the starting place. It's where it all began. It's where they landed in the Promised Land after forty years on the desert sea. The tape is being rewound. The whole nation is going back to where it all began, and being baptized, which means they are being renewed, refreshed, and ready to go. They are waiting for the Messiah to lead them once again into the Promised Land. Only this time they are going to get it right. This time God is going to see to it that they get it right. God is sending the Messiah to make sure they will get it right.

To understand Jesus' baptism you begin with the geography. The River Jordan is no ordinary river. It's where Israel started. Going into it, being baptized in it, and then emerging from it, is to start your life as a nation, or as an individual, over again.

John the Baptizer is there. His work is finished now. Everybody is baptized. They are standing around now, waiting. They are ready now. Only one thing missing: the Messiah. Hold everything. Here he comes. "In those days Jesus came from Nazareth of Galilee and was baptized by John in the Jordan."

Now here's what happened next, according to Mark. "And when he came up out of the water, immediately he saw the heavens open, and the Spirit descending upon him like a dove, and a voice from heaven saying, 'Thou art my beloved Son. With thee I am well pleased.' " That's it. Only Jesus saw it, and only Jesus heard it.

I guess everybody else went home disappointed, saying, "Did you see anything?" "I didn't see anything." "I saw this man walk into the water. I saw John dunk him down there. Then the man came up and wiped the water from his face, pulled the hair back from his eyes, headed out toward the desert. That's all I saw. If he's Messiah, then he's headed the wrong way. He's supposed to lead us back into all of Judea and into Jerusalem. He went south. We're going north. He went by himself, all alone, out to the desert. What kind of a leader is it who goes the opposite direction of his people?"

According to Mark, nobody there saw what happened, including John the Baptizer. They were there, but they didn't see it. It was a private event, a personal epiphany, a subjective experience, a secret message — "You are my son. With thee I am well pleased."

I grant you that that is a subtle point in this story, but the subtlety *is* the point. That is where you are going to find God, at the subtle points of your story. This is an epiphany, a revelation. This is God speaking. So it means when God speaks it's going to be private. It's not going to be out in the open. There's not going to be any Super Bowl promotion, no media coverage. That's the way it was when God sent his Messiah to Israel, so that's the way it will probably happen when God works in your life as well. Do you think that you are going to get more than Jesus got? Probably not. God is probably going to come to you the way he came to Jesus; that is, mysteriously, secretly, privately, and personally. Nobody is going to see it. If you want them to know about it, you are going to have to tell them.

I was reading an interview with Frederick Buechner, the novelist, who is also a pretty good theologian. He has written an autobiography in two volumes. The interviewer was asking him why he wrote it. He said that when he hit fifty, he took stock of his life and came to the conclusion that the place where God speaks, if he speaks anywhere, is in what happened to us. So, he said, "listen to your life."

That's good advice. In fact, it's the advice that Mark is giving us. "Listen to your life," because God acts privately, personally, secretly, in the sense that nobody else knows about it, nobody else sees what you see, nobody else hears what you hear.

Buechner advises us to capture the experience. Write it down. This is the way writers do it, he says, and you ought to do it, too. Get a notebook and write it down, the way writers record scenes or conversations, things that they don't want to forget. So much of life passes by unnoticed, but even more of life passes by and we forget it. So write down those special moments. Make a spiritual autobiography, and then go back to it and examine the details. Look at the subtle things. Look at the subjective feelings. Look at the things that you felt but nobody else did.

I was given a picture of my father taken about 1917 or 1918, I imagine, because he's wearing the uniform of the

United States Army in the First World War. He had only been in this country by that time for maybe five years and had enlisted in the army. He's on his way to Europe, to France where he will be wounded fighting for his new country. This picture was taken, I think, in front of the home of his parents, who had recently come to this country.

He's standing there, posing really, the way they used to do in those days. They didn't just take pictures, they posed for pictures. He's looking into the distance, his foot on the running board of a grand old touring car. The body of that car is so shiny that you can see reflected in the side of the car the curb and the lawn and something of the house. I don't know if the car is there as a prop for my father, or my father is there as a prop for that beautiful car. It's a marvelous car.

In this picture, above my father's head, is a rectangular object. It appears to be falling. It looks like nothing in particular, rectangular in shape, maybe an inch long and a quarter of an inch wide. I'd like to say a dove is descending on my father, which would be a marvelous way to end this sermon. But it doesn't look like that at all. It looks more like a stick of gum. At any rate, it's falling, and heading right for his head.

The reason I mention this is that the man who blew up the original print said that that object cannot be seen in the original print. And what's more, he said, it's not a flaw in the paper. They made several prints. It's not from a speck on the lens. It's not anything you could think it might be. It wasn't in the original print, at least you couldn't see it in the original print. But when they blew it up and magnified it, there it was.

I thought immediately of Antonioni's film, *Blowup*. Remember it? The photographer suspected something, so he blew up the print until he saw what he suspected. It was in the background, in the bushes, the once invisible, but now unmistakable face. Somebody had been there all along.

Doing what Buechner suggests, examining your life that carefully, writing it down, is to self-examination what enlargement is to photography. Recording events magnifies them to the place where you can see things in your life that you didn't notice before. You can see things that you only sensed were there. When you have the feeling that something strange or mysterious has happened to your life, and you don't know what it is but you know that something is different — blow them up, study them, and maybe you will see the evidence that someone else, otherwise invisible, was there all along. Maybe you'll even see something descending upon you, something like a spirit, which explains that feeling that you were not alone, or that feeling that came to you one day that everything is going to be all right.

Examine your life. Look at the details. Look at the subtle points. Your life from a distance is just like everybody else's life. We all look alike from a distance. But up close you can see the differences. You can see the subtle points that make each one of us unique.

Isn't it true, then, that God, who is personal, will come to you personally, and even privately, and secretly, in a way that no one else can see, and perhaps in a way that no one else has quite experienced until you experienced it?

Clare Booth Luce wrote about her Roman Catholic conversion. She said:

> *I find it difficult to explain what did happen. I expect that the easiest thing is to say that suddenly something was. My whole soul was cleft clean by it, as a silk veil slit by a shining sword. And I knew. I do not know now what I knew. I remember, I didn't know even then. That is I didn't know with any 'faculty' . . . But whatever it was, I knew it was something that made enormous sense . . . Then joy abounded in all of me, or rather I abounded in joy.*

Clare Booth Luce is a good writer. She has that advantage, but I want you to see that even with that faculty, she has difficulty describing what happened to her, because it is always so private, unique, mysterious, new, so personal, not quite like what anyone else has ever experienced, and therefore, ineffable. Just a fleeting reality, a hint perhaps, something subtle. "Suddenly something was," she said. "I knew, though I didn't know. Only it made "enormous sense." And then joy.

She presents a wonderful image of joy. She says she felt as if she were "a speck of dust dancing in a shaft of sunlight." That's the way she described her moment of epiphany, when God spoke to her.

Do you know how Mark described the same experience when it happened to Jesus? They all report this, so Jesus probably told them that this is what it was like. "It was as if the heavens opened, and a voice said to me, 'You are my son.' Then the Spirit touched me so gently, it was as if a dove had lighted on me." And that was it. And no one else saw it. It was private, personal, and secret.

So listen to your life. It will happen to you the same way, only different.

What Are You Looking For?

You have heard of "famous last words." In this text we are going to look at the famous first words of Jesus according to the Gospel of John. In literature first words are important because they are used to reveal the personality or the character of a person. In Jesus' case, they are also used to reveal the nature of his mission, whom Jesus has come for.

Jesus' first words, according to the Gospel of John, are: "What are you looking for?" revealing that Jesus has come for seekers, for those who are looking for something in this world.

It's a wonderful scene. Once again it involves John the Baptizer. We can't seem to get rid of John. He's been around the church now for about two months, ever since the beginning of Advent. Here he is again, appearing with two of his disciples.

The previous day he had baptized Jesus in the River Jordan. It was then that John the Baptizer had recognized Jesus as the Messiah. He had called him "the Lamb of God who takes away the sins of the world" and said some other nice things about him.

This is the following day. John is still at the Jordan, but now that he has baptized the Messiah, his work is over. He is ready to go. He is picking up things, breaking camp. Two of his disciples are helping him. Jesus walks by. John stops, pokes the two disciples, points to Jesus, and says, "Behold the Lamb of God."

Whereupon the disciples of John the Baptizer leave him and follow Jesus. Jesus, sensing that somebody is following him, turns around and asks, "What are you looking for?" They ask him, "Where are you staying?" a code phrase that indicates that they want to learn from him, they want to ask him some questions. He says, "Come and see." They stay with him for one day and are convinced. One of them, Andrew, who is Simon Peter's brother, goes to Peter, and says, "We have found the Messiah."

That's the way it happened, according to John. The other gospels will disagree. According to the other gospels, Jesus called his disciples from the Sea of Galilee, and they were not disciples of John the Baptizer; they were fishermen.

But this is John's version, and John draws it this way for a purpose. He wants to suggest how seekers will come to Jesus. Seekers are likely to respond to another seeker saying, "I have found something. I want you to come and see."

That is sometimes called "come and see" evangelism. You notice that it does not call you to convict anybody of their sins. It doesn't call for you to warn them against "the wrath to come." It doesn't call you to coerce or cajole or con anybody. It says that all you should say to your brother, or to your sister, or to your friend, your neighbor, a colleague, or to somebody who works beside you is "Come and see." That's all.

I like that. I like it because it reminds us that we don't convert anybody; God is the one who does the converting.

Our job is to point the way and then get out of the way. To go around talking about converting people all the time displays, I think, a kind of arrogance repugnant to many people. That's why I prefer a different vocabulary, the vocabulary of the pilgrim, or the seeker, for I believe we are all seekers. We are all explorers. Some of us may have found the treasure, or maybe only a clue. If so, we are to say, "Come and see." That's all. "Come and see."

It is possible to seduce people with promises. It's possible to scare them with threats. It's possible to subdue them with arguments. Churches, I am sorry to say, do that all of the time and call it evangelism. But that isn't evangelism and it doesn't result in conversion. Conversion is not the result of manipulating people with technique; conversion is the result of an encounter with God.

Each person will come to that differently, and the chances are that seekers will come in their own sweet time and according to their own needs. Seekers will not come because it is what everybody is doing. They are more likely to do the opposite. They are seekers because they are inner-directed. All you can do with a seeker is say, "Come and see," and leave the rest to God.

I want you to consider that that is exactly what Jesus is doing here. He is addressing seekers: "What are you looking for?"

Have you noticed that in the first four chapters of the Gospel of John, three of the four major scenes are Jesus' encounters with seekers? The first one you have just seen, with the disciples of John the Baptizer. The second chapter in the Gospel of John is the enigmatic but beautiful wedding feast at Cana. Then the third chapter is the encounter with Nicodemus. Nicodemus, a member of the establishment, is supposed to have it made, but he knows in his heart that he doesn't. He's supposed to have all the answers, but he knows that he doesn't. He can't let that be known. They would be

73

shocked if they ever thought that Nicodemus didn't have all the answers. So he comes to Jesus by night when nobody can see him. Nicodemus is a secret seeker.

Then the fourth chapter relates the encounter with the woman of Samaria, the woman at the well. She's a seeker, too, only this is a chance meeting. She ran into Jesus. But after their brief conversation she is convinced that he is the one she has been looking for, only in the wrong place. In fact that's the point of all of three encounters — Andrew, Nicodemus, and the woman of Samaria — they are all seeking the same thing in the wrong place. Jesus is the right place. That's the point of the Gospel of John. Jesus is the right place to find what you are looking for. So, "Come and see." In fact, you know what the Samaritan woman did when she left Jesus? She went back to the city and said, "I think I have found what I am looking for. Come and see."

So we see three people, all seekers coming to Jesus, all coming on their own terms, all coming with questions of Jesus. Is John revealing that Jesus loves the seeker? Is he trying to tell us that there is room in the church for seekers?

There are people who put that bumper sticker on their car, "I found it." Which is all right, but reveals that they are not seekers. It sounds like they are settlers. It sounds like they are saying, "I have arrived. I'm not moving any more. I have found it. My journey is over."

I have also seen bumper stickers with a star of David that say, "I never lost it." I like the sense of humor, and the theology. It implies that the Jews, who were given a Covenant by God, never lost it because God keeps his promise. That's biblical, and I believe it.

But I'm really uncomfortable with both stickers, because both of them imply a certain settler's smugness. If I were to suggest a bumper sticker, I think it would be, "I will always be searching." As Tolstoy, a notable Christian, said, "Life poses such great questions for us that we should never stop searching for the answers to them." Which is to say that God structures our existence as human beings in such a way that we are supposed to be searching, exploring, asking questions.

To be a Christian does not mean that you stop searching. Becoming Christian doesn't all of a sudden give you all of the answers. To be a Christian means that you have made the decision to follow Jesus whether you have the answers or not.

All that having the answers means, perhaps, is that you have the capacity to memorize a catechism. Having the answers may mean that you haven't had an experience that raised questions bigger than your present knowledge. Or maybe having all the answers simply means that you know how to fake it.

I don't know where it says anywhere that the Christian faith means having all the answers. What the Christian faith means is following Jesus, sticking with him. There are those who have all of the answers who are not about to do that, and there are those who have all of the questions who do that daily.

I had a wonderful model for this when I was a young man in college. My father was dying of cancer, and I came home to visit him. Bishop James C. Baker called and asked if he could come over and visit. Bishop Baker was an old man then, retired. Only weeks before the Bishop had lost his own daughter to cancer, yet he came to visit my father. My father got out of bed to receive him in the living room. I was invited to stay.

Bishop Baker was an uncommonly gracious, remarkable selfless human being. If you knew him you would not be surprised to learn that in the midst of his own sorrow he would come to bring strength to somebody else.

That visit made a lifelong impression upon me. I heard a wise and saintly man, noted for his spiritual depth, confess,

"I don't know why these things happen. But I believe that someday I will."

In that humble confession of faith I learned that faith doesn't mean having all the answers. It doesn't mean you will know everything. Faith means that you can have questions and still follow Jesus. In fact, I believe that is the best definition of faith: courage to follow Jesus without having all the answers.

Later I discovered that Paul said something similar to the bishop's confession in 1 Corinthians 13: "Now I know in part, then I shall understand fully, even as I have been fully understood." "Now I know in part . . ." Knowing in part is the human condition. Paul says that that doesn't change when you become a Christian. What you get when you become a Christian is not information, but faith and hope and love, and the greatest of these is love. The surest test of a follower of Jesus is not that they have all of the answers, but that they have love. As when an old man, heart breaking over his own loss, hears about a friend in pain, so he comes, without answers, but with faith, hope, and love. And from the perspective of a young man who watched all that, the most meaningful, the most important was that love, the love that forgets the self and reaches out to the other.

So I wondered as I read this text, what did Andrew hear or see in that twenty-four-hour period that he spent with Jesus? There is no record of a meeting. Did he have all of his questions answered? I doubt it. The Gospels indicate that Jesus had a terrible habit of throwing the question back at you, or he would think up another question to ask you. Most of the time he wouldn't answer questions at all.

I would imagine that Andrew returned with something greater than answers to questions. He found a life so much at one with God that he knew that it was what he was searching for. It was all there, incarnated in one life, as if God himself were with us. It came to him that he wasn't really searching for answers; he was searching for life. And here it was, embodied in a human being. Here it was before him. This is the way he wanted to live. This is the way he knew that all people are supposed to live. So, he said, if I stay with him, if I follow him, then maybe I will find the same life that I see in him.

That's why Jesus said to Andrew, "What are you looking for?" "Come and see." Jesus didn't come to give us answers; Jesus came to give us life. That's why Andrew went to his brother Simon Peter and said, "I have found the Messiah." And that's why Nicodemus, looking for something beyond respectability in his life, came to see for himself. And that's why the woman of Samaria rushed back to the city and said, "Come see. I think I have found him."

What are you looking for? Are you looking for answers, or are you looking for life? There are answers in the Christian faith, lots of them. Theologians have devised answers to every possible question that you could think of. The largest section in any library is the section on theology. They have books with answers to questions no one has asked for centuries.

I don't know about you, but the older I get, the less having answers satisfies. What I want now, more than answers, is power to live the way I saw Jesus live his life, and the way I see others who follow him live their lives, power to live the way I know I should live my life. That's what I am really searching for. I believe that everybody is searching for that power. It is called grace. It is what Jesus invited you to experience when he said, "Come and see."

Some time ago I taught a course after which I received a gracious thank-you note from a woman who had attended the class. It was the first time, she wrote, that she had realized who Jesus really was, that he was no longer a figure in the past, but somebody who had a real impact on her life now, who had changed her life.

I was flattered with that note until I realized that there were many others who had come to that class for the first session and never returned. There were others who had come every session and slept. But there was one who had received the invitation, "Come and see," and she said, "Yes." Actually, what happened was that someone had invited her to that class. I didn't invite her. A friend had said to her, "Come and see." No, I change that. This is what happened. Someone said, "There is a class at the church. Will you come with me?" That's all that was said. But I believe in that simple invitation, there was another voice that Andrew heard, that said, "Come and see if I am not what you are looking for."

When Words Speak
Louder Than Deeds

Epiphany 2 (L)   *John 1:43-51*

If I were to ask you which is more important, words or deeds, you'd probably say deeds. After all we're Americans. We are a practical people. Americans are a result-oriented people. We believe in that phrase "Actions speak louder than words." In fact, I wouldn't be surprised if an American invented that phrase.

We did invent pragmatism. Pragmatism is the only philosophy in the world that says the truth of something is found in whether or not it works.

The folk hero in America is not the fancy talker; the folk hero in America is the straight shooter — Gary Cooper, John Wayne, Clint Eastwood — who doesn't talk about the problem; he solves the problem. In fact, the American folk hero is typically inarticulate, doesn't talk much at all. He just goes in and solves the problem. We are suspicious of fast talkers, fancy talkers, and especially of smooth talkers.

The highest tribute you can pay someone is to say, "They don't talk about their religion, they live it." We believe that actions speak louder than words.

I think one reason we believe that is because as a people we are really very religious. America has one foot planted in New England in Calvinism, and the other foot planted in Philadelphia in the Enlightenment. Ironically, it is the New England religious heritage that has contributed to the pragmatic, result-oriented side of our lives. The Puritans sought to practice the biblical idea that we are to live moral lives and build a moral society. They believed the only way to tell if a person or a society is genuinely religious is in the product of their living.

That's good old Puritan Calvinism, and Calvinism got it from the Bible. In the Bible it's clear that the deed counts, not the word. That's the message of the Old Testament, especially the prophets, who said that religious words and liturgical practices are not enough; you must also live out the ethics of religion in your life. So Amos said, "Let justice roll down like waters and righteousness like an ever-flowing stream."

Jesus preached the same message: "Not those who say, 'Lord, Lord,' " that is, not those who think talking religious language is the sum and total of being religious, "but those who do the will of my heavenly Father." And all those parables he told about stewards or workers or sons who were sent into the world to do a job. Those who are genuinely religious are those who do what they are called to do.

In the Parable of the Two Sons, one of Jesus' shortest parables, the message is as clear as it can get. The father sends his two sons out to work in the field. The one son says, "I will go," but he didn't go. The other son says "I won't go," but he ended up going. Jesus asked which one of them did the will of the father. There was no question about it. The one who acts does the will of the father, not the one who just talks about it.

If ever there was a text for "actions speak louder than words," it's the Parable of the Two Sons. That's a major emphasis of the Bible. There's no question about that. Actions speak louder than words.

But not always. There are times when words are more important than deeds. Elie Wiesel put it this way: "Words can sometimes, in moments of grace, attain the quality of deeds." Sometimes words speak louder than actions.

I know of such times. I know of spouses, wives mostly, who are the recipients of gifts, who are cared for comfortably, who have all of the amenities of life. They're surrounded with all of the conveniences and luxuries of life, given to them as an expression of love. Beautiful things. The only things they lack are the words, "I love you." Three little words. What are those three little words compared with all of these grand things, these beautiful things. What are they? Everything, if they are never heard. Sometimes words are more important than deeds.

A son or daughter, grown now, says they have never heard the words "I love you" from their father or their mother or, in some families, from either one. I read about a man in his middle years who went to see his parents. He and his father were in the kitchen, sitting at the breakfast table, drinking a cup of coffee together. He finally got the courage to say what was on his heart. "You've never told me how you feel about me."

The father said, "You know how your mother and I feel about you."

"But," the son replied, "you've never said it."

The father said, "We've always provided for you, always given you everything that you ever wanted . . ."

"But," the son pleaded, "you have never *said* it."

"I heard your mother tell you . . ."

"*You* have never said it."

Whereupon he grabbed his father by the shoulders and said, "Say it, just say it — say the words — 'I love you.' Say it."

Sometimes words speak louder than actions.

Our text is about that, and also about three little words, and how important it is to say them. The three little words are not "I love you." The three little words are "Come and see."

The text is from the Gospel of John. This is John's version of the calling of the disciples, and it differs from Matthew, Mark, and Luke. In Matthew, Mark, and Luke, Jesus calls all the disciples personally, but according to John, Jesus called only some personally; the others were called by friends or family, with three little words, "Come and see." Just three little words. Can you say them?

You know what I discovered the other day? This was news to me. There are people who are completely ignorant of the church, of religion, and the Bible. They don't know anything about those things, nothing at all; except, of course, what they see on television, but you know what that means.

This was news to me. I work in a kind of religious ghetto. Most people I deal with belong to the church. Some of them are even religious.

What's more, I was raised in the church. I've gone to church every Sunday for as long as I can remember. My daddy was a preacher, so I had to go. I not only work in a religious ghetto, I was born and raised in one. My grandfather was a Methodist preacher, my great-grandfather was a lay Methodist preacher. I'm an exotic species. I can't survive outside of the religious institution, so I don't venture outside very much.

But I did once, and you know what I discovered? There are people out there — a lot of them — who have no idea what religion or church or the Bible or Jesus are all about. Did you know that? It was a surprise to me. I thought people were not coming to church because they had chosen not to. Those are the people I know. I'm very conscious of them. One of the chores I don't enjoy as a pastor is contacting members who have fallen away. It's a very hard thing for me to do because these people have chosen not to come here any more. Some of them can articulate the reasons precisely. I don't want to listen to their swan songs, but I have to do it. Every year I have to give an accounting of every member, so every year I am reminded that there are some who have come here and seen and said, "No, thanks."

So I assumed everyone who didn't come to church had chosen not to. They had looked the church over and said, "No, thanks." But I found out that that's not the case. Most of them don't come because they've never been invited. You know what some of them think? I've heard them say this — "Nobody I know goes to church." Well, I know some people they know, and they do go to church — many of them go to this church. They're highly thought of by these people, respected, even loved by these people. They are *incognito*, however, as far as the church is concerned. They hide it.

I can't hide it. Sometimes they don't even ask me what I do. They tell me, "You're a preacher, aren't you?" I say, "How did you know?" They say, "I can tell — it's the pallor." We talk. They mention somebody's name. I say, "He's a member of this church." They say, "You're kidding!" I blow their cover.

I learned another thing. These people are suspicious of words; after all, they're Americans. They're bred to be pragmatists; they want to see results. And they are especially suspicious of religious words. They know what the Bible knows. They didn't learn this from the Bible; they never read the Bible; they just know that you can say the words and live a life that puts a lie to the words. They will tell you, these people, that they know someone who goes to church every Sunday and who lives an immoral life the rest of the week. They also know you, and everything about you. Or do they?

One way to read this text is to see it is a story of what happened to Nathanael when he met Jesus. It's a wonderful story. Jesus saw him coming down the road and said, "Behold an Israelite in whom there is no guile." A marvelous phrase. Nathanael represents the very best of the biblical tradition, this hardheaded, practical, no-nonsense, prophetic tradition that cuts right through all of the phoniness of religion and gets to the heart of the matter.

There's a kind of skepticism in the prophetic tradition. So when Nathanael heard about Jesus and that he was from Nazareth, Nathanael, who was from Cana, which is right next door to Nazareth, asked "Can anything good come from Nazareth?" I like that. There's nothing gullible about Nathanael. He's like Thomas. Notice this. Nathanael appears at the beginning of the Gospel of John, raising questions about Jesus, "Can anything good come out of Nazareth?" Thomas appears at the end of the Gospel of John, raising questions about Jesus — "I will not believe until I see." So at the beginning and the end of the Gospel here are two hardheaded pragmatists. They're result-oriented; they want to see. Jesus sees Nathanael coming down the road and says, "Behold the hardheaded pragmatist."

The text condenses what happened next. I think we can assume that there must have been a conversation of some length. We know that the other disciples spent at least a day with Jesus. Let's assume that Nathanael did the same. He spent a day talking with Jesus, and at the end of that day Nathanael said to Jesus, "How did you know me?"

Which are practically the same words that the Samaritan woman said after her meeting with Jesus at the well in the fourth chapter. You remember she went back to her town and said, "Come and see a man who knows me."

That's the way it works. You believe not when you know everything; you believe when you realize, God knows me. That's what Paul says in 1 Corinthians 13. "Now I know in part but then" [that is, some day in the future, some day at the end of history, some day in heaven] "I will understand fully, even as I am now fully understood." That's what Jesus reveals to us, that God knows us. God fully understands us. God loves us the way we are right now. As the poet Ugo Betti put it, "To believe in God means there is someone who knows me through and through, and loves me still and all." Nathanael's discovery that he is known, "How did you know me?" is followed by his confession of faith: "Rabbi, you are the Son of God."

This is the story of what happened to Nathanael when he got to Jesus. But it's also the story of how he got there. And he got there by a friend saying, "Come and see."

The scene starts before our text begins. Earlier in the chapter, two of the disciples of John the Baptizer hear what John says of Jesus, "Behold the Lamb of God who takes away the sins of the world." They're interested, they follow Jesus, ask Jesus where he is staying. Jesus says to them, "Come and see." And they do, and believe.

One of them was Andrew, Simon Peter's brother. He went to Peter and said, "I think I have found the Messiah; come and see."

Then Jesus went to Galilee, and there he met Philip, and Philip believed. And Philip went to Nathanael, and said, "I think we've found what we're looking for." And Nathanael questioned him, "Can anything good come out of Nazareth?" And Philip said, "Come and see."

That's the way it happens, with three little words. "Come and see."

In his letter to the Romans, Paul says, "How are people going to call upon God if they don't believe? And how are they going to believe if they have never heard? And how are they going to hear without a preacher?" That's the way Paul puts it, but we could put it this way: How are they going to hear without an invitation? "Come and see."

During one of my forays out of the religious ghetto, I went to a luncheon and sat next to a man who heard that I was a clergyperson. He said he had just read a book written by

Dan Wakefield entitled *Returning: A Spiritual Journey.* He was impressed with this book because it was written by Dan Wakefield, and he knew Wakefield and respected him. I had read it, too, so we had a nice conversation about it. The book is a kind of spiritual autobiography and in it Wakefield talks about going to church.

It happened when he was sitting in a bar in Boston on Christmas Eve, and someone said, "You know, it's Christmas Eve — we ought to go to church." So they did, and Wakefield's life was changed. It was a while before he went back after that, but he did, a few months later. This time he went on his own, and then he went again after that, and pretty soon he was going every week, then during the week to classes, and he's never stopped going.

He wrote about how this experience of belonging to the church has changed his life. Not only has he stopped his drinking, which was a problem for him, he also discovered a depth of meaning in worship and a breadth of caring in community that he had never known before. He knows now that he'd always been looking for this, but in the wrong places.

It's a good book. But what got me was this passage. He's talking about going to church:

> To my surprise I recognized neighbors and even some people I considered friends at church, and on a regular Sunday. I had simply assumed I did not know people who went to church, yet here they were, with intellects intact, worshiping God.

Andrew told Peter, "Come and see."

Philip told Nathanael, "Come and see."

The woman at the well went back to her village and told her friends, "Come and see."

That's the way it happens.

You know, I never thought of this before, but those three little words, "Come and see," are just another way of saying those other three little words, "I love you."

Some Good News For a Change

Epiphany 3   *Mark 1:14-20*

Our youngest daughter came home from college for a visit, the first chance we had had to talk since she began the new semester. She announced that she was studying the history of the 1960s, which came as something of a shock to me. I didn't think the sixties were far enough away to allow you to get a bead on them. It seemed just like yesterday.

In 1988, *Time* magazine had a cover story on "1968." They listed all the events that happened that year in American life, events that have decisively affected life in this country since then. Most of them were tragic events: the assassinations of Martin Luther King, Jr. and Robert Kennedy, the Democratic convention in Chicago, and the war in Vietnam, which hit its nadir in 1968. It was not a good year, 1968.

I remembered that I had a book in my library which I had bought back in the sixties. I wanted to find a quote I knew was in that book. The book was entitled *Beyond Left and Right,* edited by Richard Kostelanetz. The subtitle was "Radical Thought for Our Time," a typical sixties title. I took it off my shelf and looked at the publication date. Guess what year it was published? 1968!

It's a book of essays by people like Buckminster Fuller, Kenneth Boulding, Herman Kahn, Marshall McLuhan, Simon Ramo — experts in technology. Some of them are also called "futurists," because they could see the implications for the future in what was happening in the present, especially in technology.

It was a remarkable experience to peruse that book after so many years. For instance, in the preface the editor said:

> *Some readers may be surprised and disappointed to find nothing here on Vietnam or racial justice. But the really significant events are not those that dominate the head-lines but the changes that are occurring in technology and in our way of looking at human life on this planet.*

The book's thesis was that a new era had already begun. The full radical implication and implementation of this new age awaited only our awareness of it, our willingness to enter and participate in it.

The text for that radical statement was what I was looking for. It served as an epigraph for the book. A quote from Tolstoy. It went like this.

> *All great revolutions in men's lives are made in thought. When a change takes place in someone's thought, action follows the direction of the thought as a ship follows the direction of a rudder.*

The thesis of that book, you see, was that the new era was already begun, and when we wake up to that fact, then real changes will take place around here.

Now go to our text. It's a summary of Jesus' preaching. It was written by Mark to be a capsule, a summary of what Jesus taught. "The time is fulfilled. The Kingdom of God is at hand. Repent and believe this good news!"

To show us what the proper response to this message looks like, Mark immediately tells the story of the call of the disciples. Jesus was walking along the Sea of Galilee, saw some fishermen there, said, "Follow me." "And immediately, they dropped their nets and followed him."

The disciples' response may seem a bit impetuous, even irrational. We are apt to make life-changing decisions a little more deliberately than that. They are called "career trajectory decisions" now. We would want more time to make them.

That's the point. What is being modeled in this text is not just a career changing decision; this is an awakening to what is happening in the world. A whole new age has come upon us, a whole new beginning for humankind. Nothing less than a "new creation" has happened.

The way you respond to that kind of message is to leave what you are doing and start doing something new, something appropriate to the new age. The point is, until you start living in the new age, the new age doesn't come. That's the message of the New Testament. God isn't going to plop the Kingdom down here for us. It's not going to happen that way, at least not right away. If you're going to join the Kingdom of God, then you have to leave the past and start living in the future.

Which is the meaning of "repentance." Jesus says, "The time is fulfilled. The Kingdom of God is here. Repent and believe this good news!" If Jesus came to announce a new age, then repentance doesn't mean turning back to some old morality. In fact, in this context repentance doesn't have anything to do with morality. Repentance means stop what you are doing now, stop the way that you are thinking now, and embrace this new way of thinking about our world.

I bet that is why Mark put the call of the disciples right after the summary of Jesus' preaching, "Repent and believe this good news." Because the disciples' behavior is a model of what repentance looks like. It means stop what you are doing. Start to live as if the new age were already here.

It just may be that what is preventing the new age from coming is not God's tardiness in inaugurating it, but our reluctance to participate in it. As Jesus will say time and time again, the Kingdom is here, the problem is that you just don't see it. "Let [him or her] who has eyes to see, see."

"All great revolutions begin in thought. When a change takes place in somebody's thought, action follows the direction of the thought as a ship follows the direction of a rudder." Repentance is not some negative, life-denying gesture. In fact, repentance doesn't mean turning to a past way of thinking or doing at all. Repentance means turning to a new way. Repentance does not mean to change from what we are to what we were. It means to change from what we are to what we're going to be.

Now look at the church. In that book of essays on the future, Zbigniew Brzezinski said, "America is the first society to experience the future." That's a great phrase. You can see that the authors don't suffer from timidity of rhetoric. In saying, "America is the first society to experience the future," he was referring to the technological revolutions that were happening in those days. He was certainly right. America, because of its advanced technology, is living in the future in relation to other societies, some of which are still in the Nineteenth Century and some in the stone age. America is the first society to experience the technological future.

The same thing could be said of the church. The church is the first society to live in the future, in the sense that the church is here to model the future, the Kingdom of God. The church is to live as if the time is fulfilled and the Kingdom of God is here.

In order to get into the church, you had to repent of the past. You had to put the old world behind you, put on a new life, begin living as if you were in a new world. That was the meaning of baptism and confirmation as practiced in the early church. You put off the ways of the past, washed yourself of all that, and put on a new garment to live in a new world. As Paul explained it, "Put off the works of darkness and put on the armor of light." Or as 1 Peter says, "You are a chosen race, a royal priesthood, a holy nation, God's own people that you may declare the wonderful deeds of him who called you out of darkness into his marvelous light."

Whenever you read about the church in the New Testament it is described in that kind of language. You get the impression that although they were living in this world, they were not of this world. Though they were located in this age, they were participating in a new age. They were living as if the time were fulfilled and the Kingdom of God were already here.

How are we to do that, those of us in the church in the Twentieth Century? I think we should be realistic. Although the new age is here, so is the old. Those who go into the world to make it a better place better go armed with that kind of realism; otherwise they will end up in despair.

But at the same time, if you are going to do some good in this world, then you must have some vision and take some risks. Because if, as the futurists say, the problem is the way we think, then let's begin by changing the way we think. That's a minimum risk, and it happens to be the strategy of organizations such as "Beyond War." They realize that nothing is going to happen to end the nuclear insanity until we change our thinking about it, until we name it for what it is — insanity. The problem with being insane, you see, is that you don't know it. Somebody has to sit you down and tell you that what you are doing, the way you are behaving, means you're nuts. Stop doing it! You're going to hurt somebody.

And the church, above all other institutions in this society, ought to be the one to do that. The church ought to know that war is outmoded. Jesus told us that 2,000 years ago. So maybe if we just pass the word around, the thinking will begin to change, and when we change our thinking, action will follow the direction of the thought as a ship follows the direction of a rudder.

It's the same way with problems such as hunger and all the other ills that have plagued human society from the beginning. If, as the church, we are the first society to experience the future, then we can reveal for the world what the future looks like. We can tell them that it looks like the world of the Good Samaritan, where your enemy is now your neighbor. It looks like that scene described in the twenty-fifth chapter of Matthew, where the hungry are fed, and the homeless are housed, the sick are cared for, the prisoners are visited, and the thirsty are given cups of cold water.

It's all there in the gospels because wherever Jesus was, there was the Kingdom. We know what the Kingdom of God looks like, and we can pass the word. We can announce that we don't have to live this way anymore. There is nothing technologically dictating that we have to live this way. There is nothing economically that determines it. The only reason the world exists half-underfed and half-overfed is because we allow it.

As Rene Dubos put it, the problems today are no longer problems of technology; they are now problems of judgment. They are problems that are caused by continuing to think in the old ways when the new age is upon us.

That's why I think that the way Mark describes Jesus' teaching fits perfectly with this way of looking at the world. Jesus said, the time is fulfilled; the Kingdom is here for the taking. Repent and believe this good news. The futurists are saying that the problems we are faced with today are not problems of technology; they are problems of judgment. They are problems of decision-making. They are problems of priority.

It makes you wonder, what if the church started to live as if it were the society that experiences the future? It would mean that knowing what is possible, we would repent and turn from the way we are to the way we are going to be.

That would also be true where we face not only global problems, but also wrestle with individual problems. The message of the Kingdom is just as applicable to personal problems as it is to social issues. So I am here to tell you, "The time is fulfilled, and the Kingdom of God is at hand." You can walk away from what you are and become what you are going to be. If you want to know what that looks like, then look at this text from the first chapter of Mark. It's right there. Old Peter, his brother Andrew, those old fishermen. Jesus comes up to them and says, "The new age is here, so follow me and I will give you something more significant to do with your lives than standing knee deep in a boat full of dead fish. Follow me, and I will give you life in abundance." "And they left their nets immediately and followed him." No ifs, ands or buts, no hemming and hawing, no lame excuses. They just walked into the future and started living the life that God created them to live.

That's the way it has to happen, whenever it's going to happen. You just leave what you are doing, the way you are living, and start living the way you are going to be.

Not that it is easy. Jesus warned us about that. It may mean having to take up a cross. But it also means this: the problem in your life is not that God has arranged things in order to thwart your plan, nor is there some destiny keeping you where you are, nor are you being punished or picked on or persecuted. Maybe the problem is simply that you just haven't heard the news that God wants you to live. You can leave what you are and become what you are going to be. That's what repentance means. "Repent and believe this gospel."

So repentance is not just for those who are doing nasty, dumb, or evil things. Repentance is just as much for those who are doing nothing except sitting around, being miserable, and bemoaning their plights. Like that paralytic whom Jesus came up to at the pool of Bethesda and said, "Stand up and walk." He'd been there for thirty-eight years, waiting for somebody to put him in the water. Jesus told him that the time had come for him to stop living the way he was and start living the way he was going to be. He got up because he saw, "the time is fulfilled, the Kingdom of God is here."

Nineteen sixty-eight was a significant year for Americans, but 1738 was a significant date for United Methodists. It was the date of John Wesley's "Aldersgate Experience."

On May 24, 1738, Wesley was at St. Paul's Cathedral for the service. After the service he walked to Aldersgate Street to a meeting of the Moravians. It was there during the reading of Luther's commentary on Paul's Letter to the Romans, that he "felt his heart strangely warmed."

Commenting on this, Leonard Sweet wrote that Wesley was not sufficiently converted at Aldersgate. He pointed out that Wesley was taught by his mother as a boy "to live each day as if it were your last." Susannah Wesley taught her children that little bit of eighteenth-century Calvinist wisdom so they could lead serious lives.

Leonard Sweet said that Aldersgate, though it "warmed" Wesley's heart, didn't heat it up sufficiently to change this way of thinking, because Wesley continued to live and to preach, "live this day as if it were your last." But what Jesus taught was, "Live each day as if it were your first."

"The time is fulfilled; the Kingdom of God is here." That means a whole new beginning is here. "Repent and believe this good news."

Be Realistic

How many images of Jesus can you find in the gospels? There is Jesus the Good Shepherd. Everyone should get that. Jesus, the Lamb of God. Jesus, the crucified. The teacher. The prophet. The friend of sinners. The baby in a manger. The resurrected Lord. The one who was tempted as we are tempted. The healer. The righteous cleanser of the Temple.

We could go on and on, there are so many of them. But here's one you probably would not have named: Jesus, the exorcist. It is one of the more common images of Jesus, especially in the Gospel of Mark. In fact, it's the first image that we have of Jesus in the Gospel of Mark. The first thing that Jesus does in his ministry, according to Mark, is to exorcise a demon. Which means that if anyone had asked Mark how many images of Jesus he could name, the first one he would have listed was, "Jesus the exorcist."

The first chapter begins with the baptism of Jesus by John in the River Jordan, followed by the temptation story, then the calling of the disciples, and immediately after that, our text.

Jesus is at the synagogue in Capernaum, where they were astonished at his teaching. While he was teaching, a man with an unclean spirit came, and, in an imaginative conversation, Mark has the unclean spirit say to Jesus, "What are you doing here? This is our territory. You've obviously come here to do us in. We know who you are. You're the holy son of God." Whereupon Jesus silenced him, ordered him to come out. He did. And that was the end of it. Everyone who saw it was amazed.

That incident, like all the exorcism stories in the Bible, is told according to a formula, so I wouldn't worry about analyzing the story. What we're supposed to notice is that Mark says that the first, and therefore one of the most important, things to remember about Jesus is that he was an exorcist.

That's disturbing to me. Why would Mark do that? Maybe the answer lies in why it disturbs me. Maybe it affected people in Mark's day the same way. Maybe he made such a big deal of it because they didn't want to hear this either. I'll tell you what disturbs me about Jesus being an exorcist: the implication that there are powers in the world that I can't control. There are things bigger than I am. Forces stronger than I am. Things that I can't do anything about. Things that could, and may, someday control my life.

It's like my determination not to get sick. The flu's going around. Everybody I know is getting it, except me. I am proud of that, because I take care of myself. I have healthy habits, I'm strong; I especially like to point that out. I have positive thoughts. I can will myself into health. I do everything right . . . and then I get a blasted cold.

One of our daughters was home as I was coming down with a cold. I was complaining to her: "You know, this is the first time that I have been sick in years. In fact, it's been so long I can't even remember the last time I was sick." She said, "Nonsense, you get this every year. You're just like the rest of us."

For a while I can delude myself into thinking I am an exception to human frailties. The things that happen in other people's lives don't happen to me because of who I am, because of the kind of life that I live. My virtue, my intelligence, protect me from the things that happen to other people. Or maybe it's my hard work. I am determined to avoid the "slings and arrows of outrageous fortune" that fall on other people. And then it happens, and I learn these things can happen to me, "just like the rest of us."

You know the image of Jesus that I prefer? I prefer the image of Jesus as the teacher. My favorite passage is the Sermon on the Mount. You can memorize it and live by it. But if three chapters are too much for you to remember, then condense it into the Golden Rule — "Do unto others as you would have them do unto you." Or better yet, go to the Great Commandment, or to the even shorter version, "Love God and love your neighbor." Jesus said that you could summarize it. Now all you have to do is follow it and you will have a good life.

That's the kind of world that I want to live in, a world with simple rules that you can follow. If only you could get enough people to follow the simple teachings of Jesus, then the whole world would be a better place.

I prefer the image of Jesus as teacher because it implies that the world responds to moral, rational living. That's a world in which I have control. I can make it on my own. I want to be humble about this. It's not going to be easy. I'm not even asking that it be easy. Just a world in which, with effort, you can carve out a good life, where hard work and virtue have their rewards. That's the kind of world I'm talking about.

That kind of world is a moral world. A world where rules guide behavior. If you follow the rules, you will live happily; if you disobey the rules, you will pay the consequences. Rules that everybody can learn. Rules you can summarize with the simplest formulas, like the Great Commandment or the Golden Rule. A world where those with willpower, with character, can find the good life and choose it. Where, if I know what the right is, and have discipline, I can do it. Oh, sometimes it will be tough, so sometimes I will need not only discipline, I'll need courage. But the main thing is knowing what is required. If only I can know it, then I can do it.

That's what I want to believe; that's the kind of world I want to live in. Just say "Yes" to what is right; just say "No" to what is wrong. I want Jesus to fit into that world, and the best way he does that is as a teacher. Just tell me, Jesus, how to live, and I'll do it.

I know Christianity makes a lot over the forgiveness of sins; that's what the Cross is supposed to be all about. And I have room for that. I confess that I need forgiveness, because nobody's perfect, right? But you don't need to be perfect to live successfully in this world. It's good to have your sins forgiven, because if you don't, they're going to get in your way. They will mess up your life. So forgiveness is good.

It's also nice to know that Jesus is there as a friend, to help you when you need it. "What a friend we have in Jesus." We may need some help along the way. We may need some help "to get our lives together," or "to get back on our feet," as we say. That's the world I want to live in. Jesus, the teacher, showing me the way; Jesus, the friend, helping me along the way.

The terrible affront of the Gospel of Mark to those of us who want an orderly, rational, moral world is that Mark says it's not that kind of world, not when the first thing Jesus does when he walks into the world is to exorcise demons. Mark will say Jesus is a friend, Jesus is a teacher. In fact, that's what he's doing there in Capernaum; he's teaching. But the thing Mark remembers most about him was that he was an exorcist.

So the world Mark describes is a world in which you are not always in charge. A world where you will come up against things that you cannot control, or problems you can't solve, or burdens you can't carry, bondages from which you cannot free yourself, sorrows that you can't put behind you, diseases you can't heal, a dying you can't escape. "Just like the rest of us."

Someday, instead of being in control, you will be controlled by things bigger than you are and powers stronger than you are. You may escape this for a while. Not because you are virtuous or good or kind or smart or beautiful. You will escape this for a while because you are lucky. But some day it will rise up and knock you down or possess you or wound you or cripple you or, what is just as bad and maybe worse, do those things to someone you love; and you won't be able to do anything about it. Mark wants you to be realistic. He says that the demons said to Jesus, "This is our territory."

Look at history. We like to think that history is on an upward spiral, that we're getting progressively better every year or every decade, or at least every century. And in a way we are. Our technological power has given us the possibility for greater good than we have ever known before. But it has also given us the possibility for greater evil and destruction than we've ever known before. With each advance for humankind there's that shadow that accompanies the progress, making it possible for there to be more evil.

I remember reading about Leonardo da Vinci, who was not only an inventor and an artist, but also a prophet, a visionary. He envisioned the time when we would fly in machines called airplanes. He envisioned that we would use these machines to bring snow from the high mountains to sprinkle on the cities in the summer to cool them. Sure enough, as da Vinci prophesied, the airplane was invented. But rather than using aircraft to sprinkle snow on cities, the first chance we got, we used them to sprinkle bombs on cities.

You Haven't Seen Anything Yet

Alfred Nobel announced, "My dynamite will more assuredly bring peace than a thousand conventions. As soon as men find out that in one instant whole armies can be destroyed, they surely will abide by a golden peace." But as soon as we found out that in one instant whole armies could be destroyed, we proceeded to do it.

The eleventh edition of the *Encyclopedia Britannica* was published in 1910, just at the beginning of this century. Under the category of "torture," it says, "This subject is now only of historical interest."

We like to think that. We like to think that as we become better educated, we become more civilized, more humane. But it doesn't work that way. To a degree, it does. Education does make us more civilized. But in this century, especially, we have seen that education just makes those who are inhumane more sophisticated in their inhumanity.

On Martin Luther King's birthday, George Bush spoke at a ceremony commemorating King's life. He said, "We should continue to fight for equality and justice and freedom and peace in the years to come, and forevermore." I don't know if Bush realized what he said. It may have been political rhetoric. Politicians and preachers say things like, "in the years to come and forevermore." But that's a long time, "forevermore." "We'll have to fight this forevermore."

If he was serious, then he was saying that there is that which will always work against equality, always work against justice, always work against freedom and peace. That's why we will always have to fight it "in the years to come and forevermore." Because it doesn't go away, and nothing we can do will make it go away. It goes out of sight, it goes underground, it goes behind the scenes, but it's always there, as the psalmist says, as a "shadow" that accompanies us on our pilgrimage.

You can see that shadow accompanying us not only through history; you can see that shadow darken individual lives. There's a kind of naivete that assumes religious people are protected from the evil of this world. There is also a naivete in secularism that says there's nothing I cannot do if I work hard enough and use my brains. They're both alike, ironically, the pious and the secular, because they are both naive about the evil in this world.

I hesitate to say this, for fear of being misunderstood, but in the context of this sermon I think it needs to be said. There are those who will tell you that prayer will solve all your problems; but it won't. There are those who will say that faith is able to move every mountain; but it can't. There are some who will say that right thinking, reason, will always result in happy lives; but it doesn't. Not always.

I tell you that one of the cruelest things I know is for someone to tell a person who is in the grip of tragedy, into whose life the shadow has come, who is possessed by something that is destroying them, or an illness that will not let them get well, and they never will get well — the cruelest thing is to tell that person, "If you only had faith" or "If you had only prayed" or if you had only done this or done that.

Sometimes the shadow, the evil that is stronger than we are, just moves in to darken our lives. It strikes indiscriminately, without warning and without reason. Be realistic about that. It's a rough world out there. That's what Mark is saying.

But he's also saying that Jesus is stronger than this evil. And somehow, in ways that are as mysterious to us as the shadow of evil, the light of his presence casts out evil. That's the Good News that Mark wants to give us. Something more powerful than evil has entered the world and it has never left the world, and you can use it in your battle against evil. That's the way the Bible talks about it. The Bible talks about the Christian life as having to do battle against the evil powers, words that are strange to us until we enter the world Mark is telling about.

Martin Luther was realistic about that world, and recognized that being a Christian would mean having to do battle.

Did we in our own strength confide,
Our striving would be losing,
Were not the right man on our side,
The man of God's own choosing.

Dost ask who that might be?
Christ Jesus, it is he;
Lord Sabaoth, his name,
From age to age the same,
And he must win the battle.

We're here to fight evil when it appears in history, or when it casts its shadow over our own lives.

At some point the early Christians realized this. They realized that Jesus was not going to come back and fight evil for them. We're going to have to fight evil for Jesus.

That's what Paul is saying to the Ephesians. He says we're not always going to be delivered from evil. Even though we pray, in the Lord's Prayer, "Deliver us from evil," it won't always happen. Sometimes we're going to have to fight it. He's as realistic as Mark in what we're up against. He says, "We are not contending against flesh and blood but against the principalities, against the powers, against the spiritual host of wickedness."

Now you may not want to use that language to describe the evil in this world. I don't like to use that language, either. And I don't. But if you are realistic, you'll still take evil seriously and fight it.

This is how you do it, according to Paul. You gird your loins with truth. You put on the breast plate of righteousness. You put on your feet the equipment of the gospel of peace. And then you take the shield of faith, put on the helmet of salvation, and finally, the sword of the spirit, which is the Word of God.

There is a movement in the church to remove all military metaphors from the language of devotion. I am sympathetic to that, but then I come up against someone who is fighting addiction or disease or emotional distress or evil powers entrenched in this world, powers that never go away. It is then that I turn to Paul or the military metaphors such as in Charles Wesley's hymn, "Soldiers of Christ, Arise, and Put Your Armor On." I tell these people, the first thing Mark remembered about Jesus was that he is stronger than what you are facing. So keep on fighting.

Why the Big Secret?

Epiphany 5   *Mark 1:29-39*

When you read the Gospel of Mark, you get the impression that Jesus didn't like crowds, which is strange for a Messiah who has come to save the world. I'll tell you what is even stranger. He hides the fact that he is Messiah. When he is recognized by someone, Jesus tells them, "Don't tell anybody. Keep it quiet."

What's the big secret?

It is even more mysterious when you realize all this comes during the time of Jesus' greatest popularity, at the beginning of his ministry, when he is preaching in Galilee and the crowds are the largest and the enthusiasm the most contagious.

Mark records it in this way. "At once his fame spread throughout all the surrounding region of Galilee." Jesus was a tremendous hit. At once his fame spread everywhere. That's the testimony in the verse preceding our text. Jesus' popularity and his fame are expanding, growing everywhere.

Then follow three incidents, vignettes of his experience in Galilee. First he goes to the house of Simon and Andrew, the brothers. James and John, the other brothers, are also there. Simon's mother-in-law is in the house, sick. Jesus takes her by the hand, lifts her up, and heals her. Just like that! It's a dazzling feat. A miracle.

It was that type of thing that built his popularity in Galilee and spread the word about his supernatural powers. The crowds were getting bigger and bigger. Who could ask for anything more, especially a Messiah who has come to save the people? All the people are coming out to be saved.

Then this scene. It's evening, at sundown. They brought all who were sick or possessed with demons. Mark says, "The whole city was there at the door." That's a detail not to be overlooked. "The whole city" was there. He healed those who were sick and cast out the demons of those who were crazy. Then comes this strange verse. "And he would not permit the demons to speak because they knew him."

Why the big secret? He had it made. Even the enemy, the demons, recognized who he is. They were willing to tell everybody who he is. He is the Messiah. The whole city was there. What kind of a Messiah is it who wants to travel *incognito?* Hasn't he come to win the world over? So why the big secret?

Go to the next scene. He continues his strange behavior. "A great while before day," it says, "Jesus went off by himself." Peter found him. Simon, as he's called at this point in the gospel, "chased him down." That's the literal translation of the Greek word. He abruptly and rudely came upon Jesus as he was praying and says, "I'm glad I found you. Where have you been? The whole countryside is abuzz with the news about you. It's the crack of dawn but everybody is up in Galilee walking around, looking for you. You're on a roll, Jesus. It's fabulous! You're the biggest thing ever to hit Galilee. Bigger even than John the Baptizer. So, come on! They're all waiting for you. Everyone in Galilee is searching for you."

And what did Jesus do? He said, "It's time for us to go someplace else." He turned his back on the crowd, gave up all of that fame, all of that success. When everyone is looking for him, he leaves. And when somebody recognizes him, he says, "Keep it quiet. Don't tell anybody."

Well, you can see why people wondered about the Gospel of Mark. What's Mark up to? Why the big secret about Jesus? What is Mark trying to tell us?

The first, and most obvious message, is that Jesus didn't like crowds. Wherever he went the crowds were enormous. There are ten verses in this text. In the ten verses there are these three descriptions: "His fame spread everywhere." "The whole city came out to see him," "Everybody in Galilee is searching for you." And he walks away from all that. He turns his back on it. It's obvious that he didn't like crowds.

Which ought to say something to us who follow him today. Maybe Mark, in writing the story this way, is giving a warning to the church about success. How many of us assume that the standards for success in the world are applicable as standards for success in the church?

How do you measure success in the world? You measure it by volume of sales. You measure it especially by the attendance of crowds. By the standards of the world, a crowd is always a success. I can't think of any institution in this world that doesn't want a crowd. We all want crowds, even in church. There isn't a preacher in this world who doesn't want a crowd. In the world, a crowd means you are a success.

But think of what a crowd means in the Bible. Take the word "crowd" and look it up in the Bible. In the Bible, "crowd" has a different meaning. In the Bible, "the crowd" is what Jesus tried to get away from. In the Bible, "the crowd" are those who want to use him, not follow him. In the Bible, it will be "the crowd" that on one day will sing, "Hosanna! Blessed is he who comes in the name of the Lord!" and on the next day will shout, "Crucify him!"

107

That's what a crowd means in the Bible. Crowds in the Bible are not signs of success. Crowds in the Bible are the signs of the fickleness of the world. Maybe that's the reason for the secret. Maybe Mark is telling us, "Don't make popularity a sign of success for the church." Crowds don't follow Jesus. Crowds use Jesus.

Or maybe Mark is telling us that Christianity is not to be equated with show business. It's precisely those deeds which could be labeled spectacular that Jesus is the most uneasy about. Oh, he does them. Mark says he comes casting out demons and performing miracles. But then he adds, whenever he did them he said, keep it quiet. Don't tell anybody.

So he's obviously not interested in being a miracle worker. That's not why he came. He does not want to win us over by dazzling us with supernatural power so that we have no choice but to bow down and worship him. That was a temptation, you know. In fact, that was literally "the temptation," what the temptations in the desert were all about. You remember, the devil tempted him to turn stones into bread and to jump off the height — spectacular feats of supernatural power which he rejected.

The argument for saying "yes" was cogent enough. In fact, I have heard that argument many times. Why doesn't God intervene and wipe out disease? Why doesn't God do something to end hunger? Why doesn't God do something spectacular to make unbelievers believe? Why doesn't God do something to make my life better? I would believe if God would do something. The world would believe if it could see something.

The temptation of Jesus was to equate satisfying the crowd with the fulfillment of his mission. Maybe Mark knows that the church is going to be faced with the same temptation. We are going to be faced with the temptation to confuse the will of God with the attention of the world.

Phil Donahue, in his autobiography, tells of the time he was starting out as a young television reporter and was sent to cover a mine disaster. It was late at night. Snow was on the ground. It was freezing cold. The rescue team was down in the mine shaft. The worried relatives and friends were gathered at the opening to the mine, waiting anxiously for some word of hope.

Someone began to sing, "What a friend we have in Jesus . . ." Other people joined in the singing, ". . . all our sins and griefs to bear . . ." Still more voices joined in, ". . . what a privilege to carry everything to God in prayer."

Then it was quiet. A minister stepped out of the crowd and said, "Let us pray . . ." It was a brief but very moving prayer. Donahue said it was such a moving scene that he got goose bumps. The only problem was that it was so cold that the television camera froze; they couldn't use it. Donahue held the camera against his body, rubbed it to get it functioning. He got it working, went to the minister, asked him to repeat that prayer. The minister said, "No." Donahue said, "I'm a T.V. reporter. I represent 260 stations. Millions of people will be able to see you and to hear that beautiful prayer." The minister said, "No." Donahue said, "Maybe you didn't understand. I'm not representing some local T.V. station. I'm with CBS. The whole nation will be able to see this." The preacher said, "No," turned his back and walked away.

Donahue was dumbfounded and furious. He couldn't understand it. But, he said, about a year later it hit him. He wrote that he realized that he was witnessing something called "integrity." He wrote: "The man wouldn't showbiz for Jesus. He wouldn't sell his soul for T.V., not even for national T.V., not even — praise God — for CBS."[1]

"They're looking for you," Simon said to Jesus. "They are all here. They are all looking for you. The whole countryside is here looking for you. You're a hit!" It was precisely then that Jesus said, "Then we'd better be moving on." Christianity, you see, is not about show business.

Here is another reason for the secret. It's obvious if you read the gospel. It's there for everybody to see. You can't miss it. It says, if you really want to know who Jesus is, you won't discover it in Galilee with the crowds, but in Jerusalem at the Cross.

He says that throughout the Gospel. Who he is is revealed not in his healings and his exorcisms. Who he is is revealed in his suffering and his dying.

Then he drives it home. He says, "If you want to be my disciple," which means, if you want to know who I am, "then you will take up your cross and follow me to Jerusalem." There were not a lot of takers. Not then, and not now.

I read an article written by Virginia Owen, who teaches English at Texas A & M. She said that she assigns her students to write an essay on the Sermon on the Mount. Texas is in the Bible belt, and most of her students come from middle class, respectable, conservative Christian homes, so she thought she could get away with that — assigning an essay on the Sermon on the Mount.

What she got back was a surprise to her. What she got back was anger. Someone wrote, "The Sermon on the Mount is stupid." Another wrote, "It's the dumbest thing I ever read." Another said, "It made me feel bad." Another said, "It made me feel bad because I had to be perfect. No one is perfect."

Owen summarized their reactions as being not intellectual agnosticism, which is what you would expect from sophomores in college. It was, she said,

> . . . *down home hedonism, the real article, the kind of thing that Jesus encountered in the last days of the Roman Empire in the first century. The hedonism that wants to be served, that wants pleasure in all things, that sees sacrifice*

as an evil, and a disciplined life as useless. A hedonism that knows nothing of sacrifice for a higher goal, much less giving your life in order to find it. That knows nothing of going out of your way to help somebody else, much less going the second mile. That knows nothing of a demanding ethic, such as 'The Ten Commandments,' much less an absolute ethic like 'The Sermon on the Mount.'

Owen is convinced that we're back in first-century times and that it is now the way it was then. So, she says, forget all these statistics about church growth in the Bible belt. Forget all the talk about conversions. Forget all the talk about how many people in the United States believe in God. Forget all the talk about the United States being a Christian nation. What we've got, she said, is people who are waiting for spectacular miracles to solve their problems and make life easier for them, assist them in reaching their goals, and support them in what they want to do and not require anything from them.

And here comes Jesus. They flock to him because he seems to be what they are looking for. He is reputed to have supernatural powers. He can work miracles, and they want that. So the crowds come. They want to make a deal. You give us what we want, and we'll give you what you want. You give us miracles, and we will call you "Lord." "And he turned his back on them and went on to the next town."

Why the big secret? I think Mark wrote this gospel for us. We are the ones who know the secret. That is what it means to be the church — we know the secret. We know who he really is. Paul defined the church in that way for the Corinthians. Paul said that to be the church means that we possess a great wisdom, a wisdom hidden from the world. A big secret. It's a secret because the world doesn't understand it. To the world the Gospel appears as foolishness, which is exactly what those students in Texas said it was. To the world the Gospel always appears to be stupid.

So Mark knows that the temptation for us will be to make Christianity acceptable, to make it conform to the world's standards of success, to "give them what they want." Isn't that the code of show business? "Give them what they want." In fact, is that not the rule of all business? "Give them what they want." But it is the death of Christianity.

Do you know what it looks like, authentic Christianity? Jesus drew pictures of it so we know what it looks like. They are called "parables." There isn't a parable that includes a crowd. Never does Jesus hold up a large gathering of people and say, "Behold the Kingdom of God."

You know what he says the Kingdom of God looks like? It looks like one woman calling on a sick friend. It looks like a widow giving of her resources in stewardship. It looks like someone forgiving an enemy. It looks like a Samaritan on the road to Jericho stopping to help a wounded Jew in a ditch.

A man was confronted by one of those aggressive Christians who buttonholed him and asked, "Are you a Christian?" The man stopped and thought for a moment. He said, "I really don't know." Then he took a piece of paper and a pencil and wrote some names on it. He gave the paper to the questioner, and said, "Here. These are the names of people. This name here, the first one, he's a member of my family. This next name, he's a business associate. The last name, she's my neighbor. Ask them if I'm a Christian."

Christianity is not about crowds coming to Jesus. Christianity is about following Jesus.

The Mystery of Healing

Our text, about the healing of the leper, presents us with a dilemma. The dilemma is found in these words, "If you will, you can make me clean."

That's all well and good in this story, for in this story Jesus says to the leper, "I will. Be clean." And immediately the leper left him and was made clean. That's all well and good, fine and dandy. The dilemma arises when someone, say somebody in a hospital bed today, says, "Jesus if you will you can make me well," and they don't get well. That's the dilemma.

Does it mean that Jesus didn't will it, or that God doesn't want it? Does it mean that neither one of them heard it? Does it mean that there is something wrong with the person asking for it? What does it mean when the prayer for healing isn't answered?

Maybe if we don't get well the problem is with us. God wills it but we don't, not really. I've heard that. In fact, a whole lot of people talk that way today. I read that best-seller by Dr. Bernie Segal entitled *Love, Medicine and Miracles.* It was on *The New York Times* Best Sellers list for about a year in paperback, longer than that in hardback. Working on this text, I was motivated to read it, and I discovered that Segal's book is one of those that says healing is pretty much up to you. He discovered the link between mind and body, and he explores all of the wonderful possibilities of living healthier lives through positive mental attitudes.

He has some wonderful concepts in this book, like "healing partnerships," how patient and doctor should both take responsibility for the healing, and (I like this one) how the patient should stick it to the doctors, hold them accountable. He also says that doctors ought to recognize that patients are not just medical problems but persons with feelings and fears, joys and sorrows. Doctors should consider the human dimension in healing — and how emotional support aids in healing, and even humor, as Norman Cousins pointed out in that famous book, *Anatomy Of An Illness.*

Segal says that he even discovered that music aids in the healing process, so he plays music in the operating room, but he discovered that some music is inappropriate in the recovery room. If a patient wakes up to the sound of harps, they may wonder where they are. They don't play harp music in the recovery room.

He said one time he was removing a benign tumor from a patient; it was a minor surgery, so he used a local anesthesia. The patient, therefore, was conscious. The taped music in the operating room was Frank Sinatra singing, "All of me, why not take all of me?" — which caused a little anxiety on the part of the patient.

Segal's book is more responsible than some others in that it says that proper mental attitude, emotional health, will affect the process of healing, but that it won't completely control the process of healing. Happy thoughts are not going to keep you from all disease, but they will help. They are not going to cure every ailment, but they will aid the healing.

Segal is also realistic enough to admit that one day all of us, every one of us, will get a disease from which we will not be cured. So far there are no exceptions. But, he points out, you will still live longer, and even with a terminal disease you will live more positively and lovingly, with a proper attitude.

So for Segal, it's pretty much up to you. He talks about "exceptional patients." Exceptional patients are those who discover within themselves the power of healing. But look at the implication. If you say that the power for healing is within you, then you are not far from saying that the *decision* to be healed is within you. "Lord, if you will, you can make me clean." So if you are not healed, does it mean that either the Lord was unwilling or you were unwilling?

I have to admit that sometimes it means the patient is unwilling. I've seen those who don't want to get well, and so they don't. It's pathetic when you see that. They felt either consciously or unconsciously that what happened to them was some sort of fate, so they felt there was nothing they could do about it. They just accepted it. It's pathetic when you see that, but it happens. I think they die because they don't want to get well.

But I've also seen many others who wanted to live more than anything else, who did not deserve what happened to them, who didn't will it, who had positive thoughts all of their lives, who held no repressed anger that was being manifested in the disease, who had healthy, loving relationships with other people, who had an emotional support group, who had people praying for them and who prayed themselves to God for healing, and who had a wonderful, beautiful, personal relationship with God — and they still died. They couldn't control their healing. The disease swept over them like a wave, and nothing that anybody could do could stop it.

And if anybody said, and I have heard some people say this, there still must have been something wrong in that person, something that you don't know about, something that they kept secret, something they repressed or suppressed in their lives, then I am tempted to let loose my anger at that person and respond, "How can you be so arrogant or cruel to say of anyone innocently suffering, 'There must be something wrong with you, or this would not have happened'?"

The fact is that some suffering is inevitable, and some suffering is controllable, but an awful lot of suffering is a mystery. We just don't know why it happens.

We could say the same thing exactly about healing. Some of it is inevitable, and some of it is controllable, but an awful lot of healing is a mystery. We don't know why it happens in some and not in others.

I choose that word "mystery" purposely, because a mystery is something that is beyond our control. A mystery is not something that we can make happen at our will. A mystery, like the Holy Spirit, is something that comes and goes as it wills, and we don't know the reason for it. A mystery, most of all, is like a gift. There is no given reason why it must happen. The fact that it happens at all is a mystery.

There's a law in physics called "entropy" that says that all matter is wearing down. Because of the law of entropy we could say that all life, all matter, all creation is wearing down, so it is natural for life to break down, to disintegrate. But it doesn't, not always. Sometimes life is recreated and renewed and healed. There's a power that is tearing things down. But there is also a power that is building things up, that can reverse the process of decay and create new life. We call that power healing.

The point I want to make is that there is no reason why that power should be there, but it's there. It's there sometimes predictably, so we can say with confidence to somebody, "You're going to get over this; you're going to get well. So go home, go to bed, get a good night's rest, and tomorrow you're going to feel better."

It is there sometimes unpredictably, when in a person's life all we see is disintegration, and all of a sudden the decay stops and there is regeneration. We say that it's a miracle. Why it happened, we don't know. All we know is that we did not make it happen. It's a mystery. It's a gift.

I think I know now how to interpret this text. Jesus is showing us that it is always his will that we should be well. And since we can say, "If we've seen the Son we've seen the Father," we can say it is always God's will that we should be healed. God is on our side. That's the point of this passage, and it is revealed in marvelous ways.

In the first place, look at the setting of the story. It's in the first chapter of the Gospel of Mark, which places it at the very beginning of Jesus' career. The first chapter begins with Jesus calling the disciples. Then he goes to Capernaum, to the synagogue, where he casts out demons. Then he heals Peter's mother-in-law. Then others come to him and ask him if he will cast out the demons in them, and he does. Then we come to the fortieth verse and the leper, who says to Jesus, "If you will, you can make me clean."

Look at that. The chapter alternates between demons and illness, demons and illness, demons and illness, one after another, driving home the point that illness and demons, that is to say, the presence of evil in this world, that which tears down the life that God has created, is not part of God's intention for this world. Jesus has come to drive out evil. Illness may be natural in that it is a part of the natural world, but the Bible says that though it is natural, it isn't right. Jesus is against it, and he has come to fight against it.

Secondly, look at one word in that text. The Revised Standard Version worked from manuscripts that used the word "pity," as in the phrase "moved by pity." He was moved by pity to touch the man. But some old translations say he was moved by "anger." Jesus is angry at the presence of leprosy in this world. God is angry that his children should have illness or disease or pain or suffering. God is against these things.

We don't know why these things are here. It's part of the mystery of human life. The text does not answer that question. Nor does the Bible satisfactorily or consistently answer the question anywhere. What the text before us says is that God stands against it in anger. It is God's will that we be healed. We know that. We just don't know why that will is fulfilled in some people and not in others. It's a mystery.

Thirdly, look at what Jesus does in this story. The story says that Jesus "reached out and touched the leper." That is no insignificant detail in the story. It might well be the point of the story, what Mark wants us to see. Jesus touched the leper. There was a law against that. You can look it up in Leviticus. If someone had leprosy they were officially declared "unclean," which meant they were to be isolated. It meant that nobody, not even the priest, could touch them.

So this story of Jesus healing the leper cries out to be compared with the story of 2 Kings, the story of Naaman the leper. Naaman is the commander of the army of Syria. He is an important man. The text says "He was a mighty man of valor, but he had leprosy."

They hear in Syria that there's a prophet in Samaria who is able to cure leprosy. His name is Elisha, the successor to the legendary prophet Elijah, the interior of Elijah's power through the passing of Elijah's mantle. You also ought to remember that Jesus was often compared to Elijah and Elisha, especially in relation to miraculous powers. People even asked Jesus, "Are you Elijah?"

Naaman comes to Elisha's tent and asks to be healed. Elisha not only will not touch Naaman the leper, he won't even come out of the tent to see him. Instead, he sends his servant to talk to him. He sends a servant to talk to a general! The servant tells the general, "Go jump in the river," the River Jordan, that is, "seven times, and you will be healed." Naaman is understandably insulted by all this. Imagine, sending a servant. Elisha won't even get off his prophetic pillow to go out and talk to a general.

Because Naaman had leprosy, Elisha wouldn't go near him. But Jesus, "moved with pity, stretched out his hand and touched him."

There was a story in the newspapers about Princess Diana visiting an AIDS hospital in New York City. She not only touched but embraced a little girl with AIDS, giving the world the image of royalty embracing the outcasts of the world.

This text reveals that not only does God will that we get well, God identifies with us in our sickness. God touches us, hugs us, embraces us, holds us. That's an amazing revelation. What you see in Jesus is the way God is. Jesus reveals that God is really for us. Not in any abstract way, but personally. "He reached out his hand and touched him."

If what we believe makes a difference in healing, that ought to do it. If all that we can do is prepare ourselves to receive the gift of healing, that's the best preparation we can have. Bernie Siegel agrees with this. I was pleased that in the section of his book on spiritual life he said unequivocally that the practical meaning of having a religious outlook on life is that you believe that God is for us. And if you believe that God is for us, that means that you are going to have hope, and hope is medicinal.

Bryon Janis is a world class pianist. For the last fifteen years he's been fighting arthritis. With the kind of cruel irony that life sometimes puts upon us, the arthritis has settled in his hands. For years he continued to play with arthritis, keeping his disease a secret; only his wife knew about it until he could keep it hidden no longer. During this time he practiced five and six hours a day to fight back the arthritis, but eventually his hands became so sore and swollen that he could no longer continue. He couldn't make a fist. His right wrist would only turn about forty percent. The little finger on his right hand was numb. The other fingers were beginning to fuse. In 1984 he was still playing but taking massive dosages of cortisone and pain killers.

Then he stopped playing. He retreated into his apartment and into depression. He thought his life was over. One day he stopped taking all that medicine and found himself becoming more alert and sensitive to what was happening in his life. That marked a transformation in his life. He came to terms with his condition. He said, "For the first time I could say, 'O.K., I've got arthritis. I can accept the physical deterioration but there is still so much to life.' "

He began to consider all of the things that he could do instead of performing. He said, "I could paint, I could write, I could compose, I could conduct." He said, "I couldn't control the fact that I had arthritis, but I could control how I was going to cope with it."

His doctor gave him permission to try anything as a cure as long as it didn't harm him. So he did. He tried everything: chiropracty, acupuncture, hypnosis, meditation, biofeedback, allergy testing, faith healing, diet, the whole carnival of cures. Nothing worked. That is to say, nothing cured him of arthritis. But he said this, "What helped me most is something I can't explain. I developed a personal relationship with God. I now think belief in God *is* healing."[2]

This text is here in Mark to tell you the same thing, and to encourage you to believe it.

"Lord, if you will, you can make me clean."

And Jesus, angry that one of God's children was suffering, said, "I will. It is my will that you be clean." And "moved with pity, he reached out his hand and touched him."

Incidentally, Byron Janis did get better and began to play again. A couple of years ago he gave a concert at the White House for the Arthritis Foundation. At that concert he made the public announcement that he had arthritis. He made it this way: "I have arthritis, but it doesn't have me."

Healing is still a mystery. We don't understand it. All we can do is prepare the body for it to happen. That's all doctors can do. It's their mission to prepare the body for healing with medicine, surgery and therapy. And that's all that you can do, too. All you can do is prepare your body for the gift, through faith, hope, and love.

Life Is Too Short
to Feel Guilty

Epiphany 7   *Mark 2:1-12*

The title of this sermon comes from a bumper sticker I saw: "Life is too short to feel guilty."

When I see a bumper sticker on a car, I like to pull up alongside to see if the message fits the driver. Sometimes I am surprised. I saw an obscene bumper sticker on a car driven by a little old lady. It makes you wonder what's happening to our world. Jean, my wife, saw a car with a bumper sticker on it that said, "Honk if you love Jesus." So she honked. The man extended an obscene gesture. You never know. I couldn't see the person driving the car with the bumper sticker "Life is too short to feel guilty." She was driving too fast. I couldn't catch up with her. Apparently she had no feeling of guilt about speeding.

I hesitated to use the title because it sounds like it could have come from one of those semi-religious, quasi-psychological, slick, show business enterprises that sprout up all over the place. I hate to say it, but it sounds like something that they would put on a bumper sticker. If so, I'm going to be embarrassed.

But on the other hand, what it says is true. Life is too short to feel guilty. Maybe these semi-religious, quasi-psychological, slick, show business enterprises have arisen and flourish because the church, especially the Protestant church, has forgotten that Jesus came to forgive sinners and that we are in the business of communicating that Good News. The church is in the business of seeing to it that the whole world hears that message, because life is too short to feel guilty.

Look at our text. It's that familiar story known as The Healing of the Paralytic. This story raises all kinds of questions. It says that Jesus was at home in Capernaum. I thought Jesus' home was in Nazareth. Maybe he had a condo in Capernaum. Anyway he's there, in Capernaum.

The crowd gathers to hear him. They're stacked in the house, overflowing out of the door onto the front lawn, sitting on the window sills, hanging from the rafters.

Among this crowd are some scribes. They appear here at the beginning of the second chapter of Mark, and they will reappear in every crowd scene in the gospel. Every time Jesus gathers people around him to teach, the scribes will be there taking notes, gathering evidence for the inevitable arrest and trial, sort of like the government undercover agents with tape recorders who infiltrate religious meetings in our time. They're there, in every crowd, taking notes.

Here comes a group of four men carrying a paralytic. They can't get into the house; the crowd is too big; they won't let them in. So they climb to the roof, remove a part of it, and lower the paralytic right onto Jesus' lap. Whereupon, the text says, "And Jesus saw their faith."

Now that's something. The faith that Jesus sees, according to the grammar of this text, is the faith of the four men, not the paralytic. It raises an interesting question: Will my faith help somebody else? Can faith be vicarious? I don't know. I do know that people have said, "I felt your prayers."

Or they have said, "I have been uplifted by a knowledge that you all were caring for me and praying for me." Desmond Tutu has said repeatedly that he keeps going in the fight against apartheid in South Africa because "I have people praying for me all over the world, and I feel it."

When Jesus said that "their faith" has healed the paralytic, what does he mean? Elsewhere Jesus will say, "Your faith has made you well." Is he saying, "Your friends' faith has made you well"? You think about that.

But that's not really what this text is about. Next comes a much more difficult part to deal with, and this is what the text is really about. Jesus forgives the sins of the paralytic, though nobody has said anything about this person being a sinner.

Some people point out that in those days people believed that physical disease was punishment for sin. That's true, they did believe that, and today psychosomatic medicine says, in effect, the same thing. It says we can punish ourselves physically by what we think. Evidently guilt unattended will do physical harm to a person's body. That's almost axiomatic now; we all know that.

Some people think that that's what this story is really all about. Jesus, the great diagnostician, looks at this guy and knows immediately what his problem is, why he's paralyzed. It's because he is guilty. He's laboring under repressed guilt. So he forgives him and thus heals him.

But that's not what the story says. You've got to read it carefully. The story says that Jesus forgave him his sins, got into an argument with the scribes about whether or not he could do that, and then he healed the paralytic. So there are two miracles here, separated by a dispute with the scribes. One, the forgiveness of sins, which gets all the attention in the story. The other, the healing of the paralytic, which the crowd pays no attention to except to "ooh" and "aah" as they do at every healing, whether it be performed by Jesus or anybody else. That's what they came for, to see this kind of spectacular healing.

But the healing, I tell you, was not that big a deal, not in this context. It's overwhelmed by the much more impressive and shocking forgiveness of sins. That's what got the scribes' attention. This guy falls into Jesus' lap. Everybody sees him lowered down from the ceiling. Now all eyes are on Jesus. He has to do something about this. The man is practically lying in Jesus' lap. Everybody expects a healing. The only suspense is over how he will do it. He already has a reputation as a healer. It's only the second chapter, and he's already healed lepers. That's why they're there; they like this sort of thing. It's entertainment. This guy's dumped right into Jesus' lap. What's he going to do?

Not what they expect. Not yet. They're all looking at Jesus, but Jesus is looking at the scribes, sitting there with their notebooks. Looking at the scribes, he reaches out his hand, touches the paralytic, and says, "My son, your sins are forgiven." Now notice this. He doesn't heal the paralytic; he's still paralyzed. He'll be healed later. To say, "My son, your sins are forgiven," doesn't heal the paralytic. What it does is shock the scribes, which is exactly what Jesus intended. The scribes gasp, are taken aback, shocked. They start to write furiously. Jesus says to them, "Why do you question all of this? Which is easier to say to the paralytic, 'Your sins are forgiven' or 'Rise, take up your pallet and go home'?" And then comes the punch line, and this is the point of this incident, this is why it is here in the Gospel of Mark; "The Son of Man has authority on earth to forgive sins."

I tell you, it's easier to heal than to forgive sins. All kinds of people could heal. It was a common, everyday experience. Healers were no big deal in those days, but the scribes knew that only God can forgive sins. You know what they were writing in those notebooks? "This man thinks he is God! This man thinks he's the Son of God! This man thinks he's sent here by God!"

They will remember all this and use it as evidence to get rid of him. Mark puts it here so you will remember it, too, and use it as reason to come to him. "For the Son of man has authority on earth to forgive sins." That's why he came. Because life is too short to feel guilty.

Now we're ready to look at this phrase more carefully, "Life is too short to feel guilty." Why didn't we think of that? Why don't we have a slogan like that? Why do so many people go outside of the church to deal with guilt? One reason is that they have the impression that the church is not here to get rid of guilt but to lay it on. In a sense, that's true. There are a lot of people in this world who ought to feel guilty. They have done terrible things. They have hurt people. They have thought only of themselves. They have exploited and manipulated other people. They have done things that they ought not to have done; they have not done things which they ought to have done. Guilt, in their case, is appropriate. Sometimes they even get it, and when they do, it is a most human and healthy response to what they have done.

That is the point that Karl Menninger made in his famous book, *Whatever Became of Sin?* Menninger pointed out that guilt is not necessarily a bad thing. It's the sign of a conscience, and a conscience is a sign of a moral individual, and a moral individual is a mature human being. Somebody who doesn't feel any guilt isn't really human — but sub-human. Guilt is good when it motivates change. Guilt is good if it gets you to live a life better than the one you are living now.

Someone came to a therapist complaining of guilt in their life. In the therapy it was revealed that the person was doing something that violated their sense of right and wrong. They wanted the therapist to get rid of the guilt so they could get back to the business of living the life they were living. The therapist said, "If you want to get rid of the guilt, stop doing what's causing it."

That's simple enough. But sometimes it's not always that simple. Some have stopped doing whatever it was, and they still feel guilty. Some haven't done anything wrong and feel guilty. Some go around feeling guilty for just about everything. They absorb responsibility for everything that goes on in the world, and carry that guilt around with them. For them, guilt does no good. The purpose of guilt is to stop you from doing something. But they aren't doing anything that they could stop. They're the ones who ought to hear, "Life is too short to feel guilty."

I don't know why they are that way, so I'm interested in what the psychologists say. But I don't think psychology has the full answer. I noticed something about guilt. Psychology emerged when the religious perspective of the world declined at the turn of the century. With the decline of religion, people, especially educated people, turned to the secular sciences for answers to what was wrong with them and what they should do about it. In other ages they turned to religion, and religion said that the secret of human life is to have a right relationship with God and that if you don't have that relationship you will feel guilty. In other words, if you feel there is something wrong with your life, that there is something missing, a hollowness, it is God who is missing from your life. You are made for God. You bear God's image. So you will be restless, you will be ill at ease, you will be "dis-eased," until you rest in God.

That was the religious answer to the human condition: reconciliation with God. You don't hear that much anymore. Not even in church, which is an indication of how vast has been the influence of the secular sciences in interpreting human life. Secular therapies are good; I don't knock them. I support them. I believe God uses them. I want to underscore that. But I've noticed this: When the world turned from a religious to a secular understanding of human life, they got rid of God, but they didn't get rid of guilt. In fact, if anything, the feeling of guilt has increased. Only now, people don't use religious language to describe it; they use the language of psychology. They say, "I feel depressed." Or "I feel lonely," "I feel anxious," "I feel isolated," "I feel estranged."

Though the symptoms change from age to age, the disease remains the same. A religious age will have symptoms different than a secular age, but when the symptoms keep bouncing merrily along, no matter what the age, something is seriously wrong. So maybe that old diagnosis is right. Maybe the problem is that we're separated from God, and that's everybody's condition in every age. It is the human condition.

Now get this. In the Bible "sin" is defined as separation from God, and "forgiveness" is defined as reconciliation with God. So the message you are supposed to get from religion, the reason the church is here, is to proclaim that God wants you to come home, to be reconciled, so that you can live the fullness of life you were created for. "God so loved the world that he gave his only begotten son, not to condemn the world, but that the world through him might be saved." That's the way the Gospel of John puts it. This is the way the Gospel of Mark puts it. "The Son of Man has authority on earth to forgive sins."

When Jesus talked about what that forgiveness means, what it looks like, he used the analogies of reunion, especially family reunion. I don't think that was an accident. I think he spoke that way because he knew that family was something that each one of us could understand. Even if we had lousy parents, we could understand it. Even if we came from homes that we hoped we'd never see again and have no intention of going back to, at least we know from that emptiness in our lives, or the pain, what he is talking about. We know what it should have been like like. We know what we wish it could have been.

127

I remind you also that he spoke of the Christian life in terms of family. He looked past his mother, his brother, and his sisters and pointed to his followers and disciples and said, "Here are my mothers and brothers and sisters." Here is my family, those who follow me.

And when he met with his disciples and his followers, he ate the same meal that Jewish families eat. He gathered them around the table the way the family gathers. He told us to do the same thing, because the church is the new family. And for some it will be the only genuine family that they know.

That is why I am made bold to use this analogy. A woman went through the trauma of divorce. She was the granddaughter of a Baptist minister whom she deeply loved and respected. Her grandfather had married her and her husband. She avoided seeing him, as she avoided meeting any other member of her family during that painful period in her life. After the divorce was final, she dreaded having to face her family, especially her grandfather, but she knew she had to do it. After it happened, she wrote this description of reconciliation with her grandfather.

> *I remember starting to walk up a long grassy hill to where he stood. When he saw me, he immediately started down the hill to meet me. Before I could think of anything adequate to say, he hugged me and said, "You know, I've been wondering what I said wrong." I collapsed in his arms and wept. When I finally gained control I looked into his own smiling, wet-eyed face. I couldn't think of a word to say, and he didn't say anything, either. With his arms around my shoulder, we just walked together up the hill and back into the family.*[3]

I tell you, the Son of Man has authority to welcome you back into the family.

Babette's Feast

Epiphany 8   Mark 2:18-22

It's appropriate that as we approach Lent our text is about fasting. People come up to Jesus and say, "John the Baptizer's disciples fast; the Pharisees fast; how come your disciples don't fast? The meaning of that encounter can be summarized in this simple syllogism: All religious people fast; Christians are a religious people; therefore, Christians should fast.

Jesus' answer is rhetorical and conclusive: "Can the wedding guests fast while the bridegroom is with them?" Jesus' coming is like a wedding. Who ever heard of fasting at a wedding? You're supposed to have a banquet at a wedding. You're supposed to dance and eat and drink and be happy, because the time of celebration has come.

The Gospel of Mark begins with the announcement, "The time of waiting is over, the time of the Kingdom of God is here. Repent and believe this Good News." That serves as a preface to the whole gospel. It's a summary of what Mark is going to tell about. What is to follow is good news, not bad news. The Good News is, what you have been waiting for has come.

In his parables he said the same thing in story form. A man sent an invitation to come to a banquet. All the invited guests said, "Fine, we'll be there." When the time for the banquet came the man sent the messenger again to say, "*Now* is the time, come to the feast." And no one came. They didn't come, they said, because they were not ready. They had important things to do before they could come. Things were not in order yet. Their lives were not in order yet. For them, now was the time of preparation, not the time for celebration. So the master said to the messenger, "Go out and invite to the feast anyone who will say 'yes' to my invitation. For now is the time for celebration."

It's the same message throughout the Gospel. Can the wedding guests fast while the bridegroom is with them? The message is clear and simple. Jesus' coming into the world inaugurates a whole new age. In a new age the old ways of doing things are outdated. Even old venerable religious practices, like fasting, are outdated. "You don't put a patch on an old garment." The kingdom is here. The banquet has already started.

Except there's a hitch. The text includes this line: "The days will come when the bridegroom is taken away from them. Then, on that day, they will fast." It's just like the Bible to complicate things for a preacher, mess up a perfectly good sermon. Now we have to say, "But on the other hand ..." You lose something in a sermon when you have to say, "on the other hand." But there it is.

In fact, it wasn't long before the church began to practice fasting, just like the disciples of John the Baptizer and the Pharisees. Why did they do that? Why did they take it up? Was it a bad habit they just couldn't break? Were they sneaking out behind the fellowship hall during the potluck supper, "sneaking a fast" when nobody was looking (that's called a "fast break")? Or was fasting taken up again because it was discerned to be something spiritually valuable and healthy? Is it something we should all practice?

Of course, the latter was the judgment of the church. The Roman Catholic Church practiced fasting seriously, particularly during Lent. In the Protestant tradition, less so. In the Protestant tradition it was watered down to "giving up something for Lent."

Some time ago I thought that I would leave the minor leagues of Lenten discipline and begin a fast myself. I read an article on fasting; that's what put the idea in my mind. The article talked about all the good things that fasting could do for you, how it cleaned out your system and cleared up your mind. So I decided to try it. I happened to read the article on Wednesday of Holy Week, so I thought I'd embark on a three-day fast, the last three days of Lent. It had a nice Holy Week configuration to it; I'd fast Maundy Thursday, Good Friday and Holy Saturday, after which I would be spiritually ready for Easter. After three days in a dietary tomb, on Easter I would experience something like the resurrection of the flesh on Easter.

I didn't eat anything all day Thursday; I just drank a lot of water to flush out all the posions from my system, as I was told to do. The only problem was I had to preach at the Maundy Thursday service that night. Which I did, and was about halfway into the sermon when I realized that I didn't know what I was saying. I was repeating myself. At least I thought I was repeating myself, but I couldn't be sure because I couldn't remember what I had said. Then I realized that I wasn't making any sense at all.

The congregation thought it was a typical Trotter sermon, but I noticed something was wrong. They thought, his voice is a little weak, that's all. But I tell you, I was disembodied, floating about a foot off the ground. I left the service that night and ordered a pizza! I had had my fill of fasting. I don't think I'll ever try it again.

But the church did. The church concluded that fasting is good for you. Fasting can be a valid spiritual discipline for those who want focus in their lives. That's its purpose. Any discipline is appropriate that will sharpen your spiritual vision.

But the point is that neither fasting nor denial, nor even spiritual disciplines, are what the Christian faith is all about. Joy is what the Christian faith is all about. That's the permanent lesson in this text. Fasting is permissible, but it's not the center. Christianity is about joy! Joy, because in Jesus Christ something entirely new has happened to this world. Joy, because in Jesus Christ my life has a new beginning.

Therefore, the old ways of living and thinking in the world are as inappropriate as putting new wine in old wineskins and a new patch on an old garment. With Jesus Christ the time of waiting, the time of penance, is over; the time of celebrating and the time of rejoicing are here. As Nietzsche used to say, "Christians ought to look more redeemed." Or to paraphrase a famous saying of William Sloan Coffin, if only one-tenth of what Christians believe is true, they ought to be ten times more joyful. Christianity is not about what we ought to do. Christianity is about what God has already done for us.

Most of us need to hear that, and some of us need to have it drummed into us, because after all of these years of going to church we still don't get it. If you are a compulsive, rules-oriented, over-achieving, perfectionist, type A personality, you need to hear this message over and over again, because it's going to be hard for you to get it: God loves you as you are and wants you to enjoy your life as it is.

It's too bad there's not a "Church of the Disciples of John the Baptizer" around, because many of us would be much more comfortable there. The Church of the Disciples of John the Baptizer, would be organized around doing chores, making preparations, keeping busy, trying to make everything perfect, trying to make everybody perfect for the coming of Christ. That's a never-ending job. It's a religion of perpetual preparation.

"How come your disciples don't fast like the disciples of John the Baptizer?" Because the bridegroom is *here*. Now is the time for celebration.

Holy Communion has been a platform on which this issue has been debated. What are we doing in Holy Communion? Is it a service of preparation, or a service of celebration?

I realized some years ago that I had it all wrong. I learned it wrong, and I suspected that a lot of you did, too. I learned that Communion was a service of preparation. I think I know why I learned it that way. When I was growing up in church, Communion focused on the suffering of Christ and on my sin. The point the worshiper got in going to Communion was that we were there to feel sad for an hour. Sad for Jesus and sad for ourselves, because I just can't seem to get my life straightened out. The message was that Christ keeps suffering up there because we keep messing things up down here. So try to do better. Come back next time we celebrate Communion (in most Protestant churches in those days that meant next year), and we'll hold up your life to the Cross again to see how far short you fall this time.

I think a lot of people had that experience. When I was a young pastor starting out in my first church I noticed that most of my parishioners stayed away on Communion Sunday. When I asked them why, they said, "Because it is so depressing." I saw then that we had made Communion an office of penance rather than a service of celebration, because the Communion focused on me, and not on God. It focused on how far short I have fallen, rather than how much God has given.

Communion is not about sin, not really. It's about grace. And it's not about suffering, either, even though it remembers the Cross. It remembers the Cross to remember Christ's victory, his gift to us. Most of all it is a "means of grace." That's the definition of a sacrament, the "means of grace," which means that it's an event through which God can touch you. Even change you.

You Haven't Seen Anything Yet

I saw a remarkable movie entitled *Babette's Feast*. Babette is a French woman who escapes from some unspecified danger in France and flees to Denmark. She happens upon a religious community in the desolate isolated peninsula called Jutland. The community is made up of people who, a generation before, had moved there to get away from the world and all of its temptations, much the same way the radical religious communities came to America in the Nineteenth Century to found settlements apart from the world.

At the time the story begins, the founder of the community has died, but his two daughters carry on the work, hold the community together, and continue to live in the main house in the village. Both daughters denied themselves to give their lives to their father's mission. One denied herself a singing career; the other, a marriage.

Into this dismal scene comes Babette, the Frenchwoman. The two sisters take her in as a cook and housekeeper. In time, Babette receives a large sum of money from France, which she wants to share with the community as an expression of thanks. The way she can do that best is to prepare them a classic French meal. The sisters say no immediately, because they believe that to enjoy food is to be distracted from the spiritual life. Babette insists, and the sisters relent.

The whole community is invited to the feast. There are only about twelve people left in the community. The invitation goes out to all of them, "Come to the feast." All twelve come reluctantly and resolve not to enjoy the meal since it is sinful to enjoy the things of this world.

The meal is irresistably enjoyable. They can't help but enjoy it. You sit in the theatre and look at the table on the screen and you can hardly resist it yourself. The guests can't help but enjoy the meal, but they refrain from any expression of their feeling. They reason that if they don't say anything about how they feel, they can deny it.

During the course of the meal the community is transformed. Feuds that had endured for years suddenly got settled. Wrongs harbored are forgiven. Hearts saddened by sorrow are uplifted. Spirits dampened by obligation are freed. All of this happens because they partake of a meal that was prepared for them as an act of grace, freely given, no obligation, given to them out of love. What they receive is something more than the elements of the meal. In fact, the elements in the meal become the means that something else uses to change their lives.

One of the guests is a general visiting his aunt in the village. While the others are resolved to say nothing about the meal as they eat, he's eloquent in his praise of it. He celebrates every course. He has served in Paris, so he knows good food; in fact, while eating his meal he thinks he recognizes the chef.

Finally, moved by all of this culinary artistry, the general makes a speech.

> *We have all of us been told that grace is to be found in the universe. But in our human foolishness and shortsightedness we imagine grace to be finite. For this reason, we tremble before making our choice in life, and after having made it again tremble in fear of having chosen wrong. But the moment comes when our eyes are opened and we see and realize that grace is infinite. Grace, my friends, demands nothing from us but that we shall await it with confidence, and acknowledge it in gratitude.*

That's what Holy Communion is all about. It's about grace. It's about what God has done for you, and it's about what God can do for you. It's a means of grace — grace which demands nothing from you but that you shall await with confidence and acknowledge it in gratitude.

On the Campaign Trail

The Transfiguration of Our Lord   Mark 9:2-9

The title of this sermon was chosen to give us a perspective on the text for this morning, the story of the Transfiguration. The scene comes right in the middle of the Gospel of Mark and serves as the literary turning point in the story. There are sixteen chapters in Mark. The Transfiguration comes at the beginning of the ninth chapter. Before it, for eight chapters, lies the Galilean ministry of Jesus. After it, the road to Jerusalem and the Cross.

The story of Jesus, according to Mark, begins with the baptism in the River Jordan and a voice from the heavens saying, "This my Son. With thee I am well pleased." Mark begins the story of Jesus with God choosing Jesus to be his Son, and the Messiah.

But that was a private epiphany, a personal revelation. Only Jesus heard that voice. That story is followed by eight chapters of teachings, healings and exorcisms, and encounters with all kinds of people — sinners and righteous, important people and little people — all there to provide the evidence that what happened at the baptism, that voice saying, "You are my Son," was indeed the voice of God, though no one but Jesus heard it. Therefore Jesus is really the Messiah, even though he personally denied it, or at least refused the title.

The story through the first eight chapters reads like being on the campaign trail, visiting from town to town, going from one region of Galilee into another, speaking, preaching, healing, gathering support, his reputation building, his fame spreading. It's as if he were getting ready, gaining momentum, to go to Jerusalem to claim his real title, his office as king. If he really is the Messiah, he will be crowned in Jerusalem. There he will be hailed "King of Kings," and all the kingdoms of this world would be his, and of his kingdom there would be no end.

That's the way they talked about "Messiah" in those little towns in Galilee, which were the political equivalent of the little towns in Iowa where, in American elections, the first primaries are held. At least, some were talking that way until Jesus told them to be quiet.

Now that's past. The primaries are over. The real test awaits him. This text is for the last Sunday in Epiphany. Next Sunday is the first Sunday in Lent, and with that the march to Jerusalem. The primaries are over. Jesus and the disciples have a campaign staff meeting.

That scene immediately precedes this text and is necessary for providing the context. The meeting takes place at Caesarea Philippi. They discuss the campaign. Do they have enough votes now to march confidently into Jerusalem and win the campaign? It's one of those meetings where everything comes out. Did you ever have one of those, where it's decided that we'd better be honest this time? No more holding back from the boss. Let's stop the pretending and lay it out on the table.

Jesus asked his disciples, "What do the polls say?" Which is like saying, "Who do people say that I am?" They answered honestly, "Some say that you are Elijah; some say you are John the Baptizer; some say that you are one of the other prophets," which I take to mean that nobody is saying that he is the Messiah.

Now this isn't recorded; you have to read this between the lines. But I bet you that a lot more was said at that meeting, such as, "If you are Messiah, then why don't you act like it? Why do you hide it? When people recognize who you really are, why do you tell them to keep it quiet? Why don't you do something 'Messiah-like,' like blow away a Roman garrison? Why don't you do something a little apocalyptic for a change? No wonder you don't have any votes. Three years campaigning, and you still don't act like a Messiah. That's why they think you are Elijah or John the Baptizer. They are not going to call you Messiah until you act like one."

Have you ever been to one of those meetings? Say, at the office. Things aren't going well, people are unhappy with each other, there are misunderstandings, work isn't getting done, people are complaining. So the memo goes around: "Staff meeting at 8:00 a.m. tomorrow." The plan is to get everything out on the table, just talk about it, see if we can't work this thing out and start working as a team around here once again.

It was that kind of meeting, I think, at Caesarea Philippi. All the complaints laid out on the table. "The years of campaigning . . . and Jesus, they still don't know who you are. They think you are some kind of prophet, for crying out loud. And it's all because you keep hiding who you are."

Then it's quiet. They said what they wanted to say, and now it's time for Jesus to respond. "All right. That's what the crowds are saying, but what do you say? Peter, who do you say that I am?" Peter says "I believe you are the Messiah. You are the Christ." Then Jesus warned them, "Don't tell anybody." The disciples shake their heads in despair. They can't believe it.

Jesus lays out what is going to happen next, what lies ahead. They will go to Jerusalem, where he will be arrested and tortured and killed and on the third day rise from the dead. Whereupon Peter, obviously fed up with all this, blurts out, "No! No, that's not the way it's supposed to be. That's not the way it's going to be." Jesus says to Peter, "Get behind me, Satan." Which is when the meeting broke up.

"Six days later . . ." this is our text. "Six days later," there is another meeting. This time just the executive committee: Peter, James, and John. The three of them go off with Jesus onto a mountain. It's a wonderful scene called "the Transfiguration." You have to know your Bible to understand what's happening here. It's full of symbols taken from Scripture revealing the significance and the meaning of this event.

First, Jesus is "transfigured," which means that he appears the way he will appear when he is resurrected. It is a preview of the resurrected Lord. "His garments glistening, as white as no fuller could ever bleach them," is language referring to the end — time when the will of God is finally done for all of us. So this is a wisdom of the way that Jesus is going to be at the end. He will be resurrected. He will be in his glory. He will be Lord.

Then Moses and Elijah appear, like two retired presidents, to join the winning candidate on the platform at the convention. Moses takes one of Jesus' hands, Elijah takes the other; they hold Jesus' hands over his head and with their free hands give the victory sign. It's a wonderful scene, the three of them there.

For Peter, James, and John this is a marvelous experience, loaded with significance. The Jews had a phrase, "the Law and the Prophets." There is no higher authority in Judaism than "the Law and the Prophets." If you wanted to prove anything conclusively, if you wanted to shut up your opponent and end the debate, you said, "This is according to the Law and the Prophets." Moses, the bearer of the Ten

Commandments, was a symbol of the Law; Elijah, the first of the great prophets, was the symbol of the prophets.

The meaning was clear. There is Jesus with Moses on one side and Elijah on the other. That ought to end the debate among the disciples as to whether or not Jesus knows what he is doing. Jesus must be running his campaign the right way, because there are Moses and Elijah, the Law and the Prophets, on either side of him, saying Jesus knows what he is doing.

Peter, understandably overwhelmed by all this, as usual gets it wrong and says, "Master, this is just terrific. Let me make three booths, one for you and one for each of your friends here." The construction of booths is also a biblical symbol. It was believed that in the endtime when the kingdom came, Moses and Elijah would return to set up permanent residence with the Messiah in the kingdom. Peter thought that that was what was happening here. The kingdom had obviously come, because there they were, the three of them together. So he offered to build houses for them to dwell in.

Jesus, Moses, and Elijah just stand there and stare at him, revealing, to Peter's embarrassment, that he had it all wrong.

The scene concludes with that voice again, the same voice that was at the Baptism. At the Baptism only Jesus heard it. At the Transfiguration the disciples hear it. At the Baptismit was a private event. At the Transfiguration it is a public epiphany, for the disciples, anyway, and for all of those who have doubts about whether Jesus knows what he's doing.

God says, "This is my Son," as in the Baptism. But this time he says one more thing: "Listen to him." Listen to him. Listen to him . . . the phrase bouncing off the walls of the mountains. "Listen to him." Then Moses and Elijah disappear. Jesus is left standing there alone. That's the way it ends.

It's a confirmation experience. It said to the disciples, Jesus is right. Jesus is not misguided. He is not mistaken. He really is the Messiah, and he really knows what he is doing. So, listen to him.

How are we to find its meaning for us? Look again at where it appears in the Gospel of Mark. It comes at the low point in the story. It comes exactly at that point where the effort to be a disciple becomes the most laborious and discouraging. The excitement of the beginning has worn off, and the celebration of the victory is yet to come. In fact, at this point in the story it appears that there won't be a victory celebration. It looks like it's going to end right here at Caesarea Philippi.

That's exactly where the Transfiguration comes. It's told as an epiphany, which is what it is. It's something that happened to Jesus, but it is also something that happened to James and John, and especially, to Peter. The story has Peter's unmistakeable signature. Peter commits a *faux pas* in it. He's always doing that. Peter was so venerated in the early church that only he could tell those stories about himself. So this is Peter's story.

I think it happened this way. It think he was visiting one of his churches and somebody asked him, "Peter, did you ever feel like quitting? Did you ever get so discouraged that you wanted to give up?" And Peter said, "Yes. In fact, I can remember exactly when it was. It was at Caesarea Philippi, and we were about as low as we could possibly get. We wanted him to take the country by storm, and he wanted to approach every individual in love. We wanted him to do it with force. That was our strategy. His strategy was the painfully slow strategy of loving each individual.

"So, at Caesarea Philippi all this frustration was put on the table. I got angry and said something that I regret, which prompted Jesus to say something that hurt me deeply. Later, six days later, we were together in prayer on a mountain, and it was there I saw that everything was going to come out all right. It was as if God gave me a glimpse of the end of the story. I saw what you and I know now, but I didn't know then. I saw a vision that Jesus really is Lord. And what he taught and the way he lived is really the way God wants us to live. It was that assurance that kept me going through the roughest period of my life."

I think it must have been like that, Peter remembering a terrible time. Peter, did you want to quit? Did you ever get so discouraged that you wanted to give up? "Yes," Peter said. "It was at Caesarea Philippi. And then something happened. It was an epiphany, a revelation, that gave me courage to keep on going. It was a confirmation of all I believe, an assurance that all I held onto was true."

Frederick Buechner, the novelist, said

> *As a writer I developed a sense of plot. Then it occurred to me that perhaps life itself has a plot, and that the events of our life, random and witless though they may be, generally seem to have a shape and a direction of their own, and are seeking to show us something, and to lead us somewhere.*

That's what an epiphany is. An epiphany is an event that wants to show us something, that wants to lead us somewhere. That wants to make possible something that otherwise couldn't happen in our lives.

Like another story from another political campaign, a contemporary one that was told by James Wall, the editor of *The Christian Century.* He was Jimmy Carter's campaign manager in Illinois in 1980. He says they were driving in a car together through the Illinois countryside. It was a low time in the campaign. Eight days earlier, when Carter had come in fourth in the Massachusetts primary, it had looked like it was the end of his campaign. The previous day, however, he had defeated George Wallace in the Florida primary. The next day, to everyone's surprise, he would go on to win the Illinois primary.

Wall asked Carter about that Massachusetts defeat. Carter smiled and said, "It was all for the best." Wall said, "We two Georgia boys, products of hundreds of Sunday School sessions, knew exactly what he meant."

And so would Peter. Out of the crisis, life would go on. Out of the crisis would come the Transfiguration and from the Transfiguration would come strength. That's what epiphany does. It shows us something, or it leads us somewhere, so that someday we can look back and say, "It was a terrible time, but it was for the best."

End Notes

1. I am indebted to Clarence Forsberg for this story.

2. Quoted in a newsletter published by Ray Balcomb, Portland, Oregon, Vol. IV, p. 30.

3. From *The Single Experience,* by Andrea Wells Miller and quoted in a sermon by Don Shelby, "How Sweet It Is," July 24, 1988, Santa Monica, California.